PHOTOGRAPHS BY RACHEL RIEDERMAN

ONCE UPON A RIND IN HOLLYWOOD

50 MOVIE-THEMED

**CHEESE PLATTERS &
SNACK BOARDS FOR
FILM FANATICS**

ULYSSES PRESS

Published by:
ULYSSES PRESS
PO Box 3440
Berkeley, CA 94703
www.ulyssespress.com

ISBN: 978-1-64604-409-2
Library of Congress Control Number: 2022936257

Printed in China
10 9 8 7 6 5 4 3 2 1

Project editor: Shelona Belfon
Managing editor: Claire Chun
Editor: Susan Lang
Proofreader: Renee Rutledge
Front cover design: Raquel Castro
Interior design: what!design @ whatweb.com
Production: Winnie Liu
Recipe developer/food and prop stylist: Rachel Riederman

CONTENTS

INTRODUCTION

Do you love movies? Do you love cheese? Then this is the book for you. Imagine this: you settle in to watch your favorite film and close at hand is not merely popcorn, but a perfect selection of cheeses, meats, candies, and snacks, all perfectly arranged for whatever 90- to 180-minute adventure you're about to embark on. Get ready to impress your friends, family, or followers, or just treat yourself by eating delectable and delicious cheese for dinner.

Once Upon a Rind in Hollywood highlights 50 movies that you know and love, paired thematically with cheese and snack boards (as well as some even cheesier puns). What goes better with a *Lord of the Rings* marathon than a "second breakfast"–inspired spread? Can you even watch Monty Python without shrubbery crudités nearby? Why not a *Twilight* rewatch with a selection of apple slices and salami rosettes? In these pages, you'll find a selection of Hollywood classics, cult favorites, blockbuster hits, horror icons,

and more. Some references are deep cuts while others are just plain silly, but always a fun way to pay homage to some popular crowd-pleasers. The list is by no means comprehensive, but a selection of favorites crowdsourced from friends, family, and colleagues. There's definitely no shortage of beloved '90s films on this list, but the classics are spotlighted as well!

Okay, but What Is a Snack Board?

Just as gritty antihero tales have become the hottest box office trend, snack boards have swept into our lives and social media feeds as the trendiest and most delicious way to spend an evening. They go by many other names (for example, cheese plates, charcuterie boards, and shark-coochie-boards), but at their core they are bite-size, snackable foods displayed on a plate or cutting board. They can be made up of cheese and meats or more playful treats like candy or nachos.

What Do I Need?

No special skills required for this book! While this book's fabulous photographer Rachel has gone above and beyond to make these boards look absolutely stunning, what matters most is just how delicious they taste. No time for a salami rosette? It'll taste just as good in slices. Not sure you want to make your own meatballs? There are frozen ones out there for a reason. All the recipes in this book are designed to play on the themes and ideas in their corresponding movies, but they are suggestions. Feel free to make adjustments based on your preferences (not everyone likes roquefort), what's available, and what you have time for.

However, here are a few suggested supplies for ease of eating and if you're looking to make your board social-media friendly:

• Cutting boards or large platters: This can be a cheeseboard or any flat surface that allows you to display and slice cheeses and meats on the fly.

• Cheese knives: You can't go wrong investing in some cheese knives. They have the right leverage and size to really dig in and get a hefty slice of whatever cheese you're after.

• Ramekins or other small dipping bowls: A ready supply of these is crucial for various dips, spreads, and soft cheeses.

BRIE-LIEVE IN LOVE

ROMANCE

"DRAW ME LIKE ONE OF YOUR FRENCH GRUYÈRES"

Titanic (1997)

Yes, *Titanic* was released over twenty years ago, but we will never let it go. This is a gastronomic take on the rich girl/poor boy love affair for the ages. Feel free to serve it up on your fanciest china or a rustic platter. Either way, this is one snack board that is *definitely* big enough for four, so don't keep it all for yourself (looking at you, Rose).

Serves 4

FIRST CLASS

8 asparagus spears

4 carrots

4 mini brie, halved

2 small golden beets, finely shaved

2 tablespoons microgreens or fresh herbs, chopped

½ cup good vinaigrette

4 ounces gruyère, sliced ¼ inch thick

4 apricots or, if not in season, fruit of your choice, halved and each half quartered

4 canelés or fine pastry of your choice

fine brut, to serve

STEERAGE

4 ounces swiss cheese slices

4 ounces butter almond thins or biscuit of your choice (to help with nausea often accompanying being below deck)

8 ounces dried apricots

2 cups pistachios or nut of your choice

"Iceberg Straight Ahead" Wedge

whisky, to serve

"ICEBERG STRAIGHT AHEAD" WEDGE

1 small head iceberg lettuce, quartered

1 cup blue cheese dressing of your choice

4 ounces blue cheese of your choice, crumbled

4 strips bacon, crumbled

1 pint cherry tomatoes, halved

2 tablespoons chives, finely chopped

freshly ground black pepper (optional)

FIRST CLASS

Blanch and shock the asparagus and carrots. Make an ice bath by filling a medium bowl with ice and some cold water, and set aside. In a medium pot of salted boiling water, immerse all 8 asparagus spears for about 2 minutes, until bright green and fork tender. Place into the ice bath to shock and cool. Repeat the same steps for the 4 carrots, immersing for about 3 minutes. Place the vegetables on a clean dish towel to dry.

On a salad plate, line up 2 asparagus spears and a carrot, place the brie halves alongside, scatter a few beet shavings and a sprinkling of microgreens, and lightly drizzle with vinaigrette. Repeat the steps for the remaining servings.

On a dessert plate, fan out the gruyère and fresh fruit, and place the pastry alongside. Repeat the steps for the remaining servings. Serve with glasses of chilled brut.

STEERAGE

On a dinner plate, place the "Iceberg Straight Ahead" Wedge, then fan out a quarter of the Swiss cheese and biscuits, and add a quarter of the apricots and pistachios or other nut. Serve with a glass of whisky straight up. Repeat the process for the other three servings.

"ICEBERG STRAIGHT AHEAD" WEDGE

Drizzle each wedge of lettuce with the dressing, and top with the blue cheese and bacon crumbles. Scatter tomato halves around the base, and sprinkle the wedge with chives and black pepper, if using.

THE PRINCESS BRIE

The Princess Bride (1987)

Anybody want a peanut? This cheese and chocolate board pairs brie, manchego, and gouda alongside a selection of nuts, fruit, and, of course, chocolate. The Dread Pirate Roberts (or whoever is using the name at the time) would enjoy these chocolate doubloons. And including a few peanut butter cups in honor of the fair lady played by the iconic Robin Wright was a gimme. The Miracle Max Pill recipe allows you to make your own miracle, sure to bring anyone who is "mostly dead" back to life. The chocolate coating makes it go down easier, but make sure you don't go swimming for a good hour after eating. Enjoy, as you wish!

Serves 4

THE BOARD

4 ounces manchego cheese, cut lengthwise into ¼-inch slices

4 ounces aged gouda

4 ounces French triple crème brie

Miracle Max Pills

8 ounces miniature peanut butter cups

2 tablespoons marmalade or jam of choice

handful of chocolate coins

3 ounces dark chocolate bar, broken into large chunks

2 cups peanuts in the shell

handful of raisin rosemary and pumpkin seed crackers or seeded fruit crackers of your choice

MIRACLE MAX PILLS

1 cup crunchy salted conventional peanut butter (natural is too runny)

½ cup crushed pretzels

1 teaspoon honey

¼ teaspoon kosher salt

1 cup dark or semisweet chocolate chips

THE BOARD

Fan out the manchego slices in a corner of a serving platter or board. Fully or partially chunk the gouda and add it to an opposite section, then add the brie to another open section. Place clusters of Miracle Max Pills and peanut butter cups in open sections, and add the marmalade or jam in a small jar or saucer. Scatter the chocolate coins, pieces of chocolate bar, peanuts, and crackers in the last open areas.

MIRACLE MAX PILLS

Line a baking sheet with parchment paper, and set aside.

To a small bowl, add the peanut butter, pretzels, honey, and salt, and stir to combine. Place uncovered in the freezer to set, about 20 minutes.

Scoop balls about 1 tablespoon in size and gently roll them between your hands to make a pill shape. Place on the baking sheet, spacing 1 inch apart. Place uncovered in the freezer to set until very firm, about 1 hour.

In a bowl set over a pot of simmering water, or in the microwave, melt the chocolate chips. If using the microwave, melt and stir in 1-minute increments. Using two forks, quickly dip the peanut butter pills into the chocolate, letting any excess drip off. Place back on the baking sheet. Repeat the process for all the peanut butter pills, and place in the fridge until the chocolate has set, about 20 minutes. This recipe makes 12 pills.

TIP: *Miracle Max Pills can be made a day ahead of time and kept in a sealed container in the fridge for up to a week.*

"NOBODY PUTS BABYBEL IN THE CORNER"
Dirty Dancing (1987)

The 1987 film *Dirty Dancing* has been a classic rom-com since its release, and it was the first film to sell more than a million copies for home video (if you're old enough to even remember VHS). When you feel your "hungry eyes" coming on, mambo (or pachanga) over to this board inspired by a bagel brunch at Kellerman's Resort. As you enjoy your summer in the Catskills, remember you don't need to carry a watermelon to have the time of your life.

Serves 4

THE BOARD
½ pound lox

¼ pound scallion cream cheese

¼ pound plain cream cheese

4 hard-boiled eggs, halved

4 Babybel cheeses

Assorted Accompaniments

8 assorted mini bagels

coffee, orange juice, or mimosas, to serve

ASSORTED ACCOMPANIMENTS
2 tablespoons capers

1 small red onion, sliced

1 pint mini tomatoes, or 1 medium tomato, sliced

4 mini cucumbers or ½ English cucumber, cut into chunks

1 lemon, cut lengthwise, then crosswise into ¼-inch slices

¼ cup fresh dill, for garnish and sprinkling

flaky sea salt and freshly ground coarse black pepper, to taste

THE BOARD
Drape the lox by the slice into the center of the board or serving platter. Scoop the two types of cream cheese into small bowls, and place them on the board or platter. Add the eggs, Babybel, and any accompaniments you wish to use. If using capers, place them in a small bowl on the board or platter. Place the bagels on a separate platter. Serve with coffee, orange juice, or even mimosas.

YOU'VE GOAT MAIL

You've Got Mail (1998)

Fall in love at first byte like Joe NY152 and Kathleen Shopgirl with this classic NYC-inspired board featuring everything bagel hot dogs, pretzel chips, and fresh veggies you can find at your local shop (which may or may not be around the corner). A classic rom-com with heart and sweet '90s nostalgia, *You've Got Mail*.

Serves 4

1 (16-ounce) package everything bagel dogs, cooked according to package directions

1 cup pretzel crisps

2 celery stalks, cut on a sharp diagonal, around ⅜ inch thick

3 Persian cucumbers, sliced lengthwise

3 carrots, sliced lengthwise, then cut on the diagonal

8 ounces cauliflower florets

6 ounces baby cauliflower

4 mini New York–style cheesecakes

1 (4.5-ounce) creamy goat cheese spread

½ cup Castelvetrano olives, or olives of your choice

¼ cup spicy brown mustard

1 cup mini San Marzano tomatoes or any small tomatoes

4 ounces sugar snap peas

On a large platter or board, add the bagel dogs, pretzel crisps, celery, cucumbers, carrots, cauliflower florets, baby cauliflower, and mini cheesecakes. Add small bowls of the goat cheese spread, olives, and mustard, and fill any open areas with the tomatoes and sugar snap peas.

TIP: *Vegetable prep can be done a day in advance, and the vegetables kept in the fridge in containers with some water to keep them from drying out.*

BLUE-CHEESE AT TIFFANY'S

Breakfast at Tiffany's (1961)

No one knows how to party better than a New Yorker! This recipe inspired by *Breakfast at Tiffany's* will leave you reeling to throw your own cocktail party, Tiffany included. Although there was no food in the iconic *Breakfast at Tiffany's* cocktail party, here is a recipe that will satisfy even the craziest partygoer. Enjoy the BEST PARTY EVER with the best appetizer ever, leaving your guest wanting more, more, more!

Serves 4

THE BOARD
assorted canapés or hors d'oeuvres, heated according to package directions

Goat Cheese Apricot Crisps

Blue Cheese Fig Crackers

GOAT CHEESE APRICOT CRISPS
4 ounces chèvre

1 (4.5-ounce) package rosemary crisp crackers

4 fresh apricots, halved and each half sliced into eighths, or apricot preserves

1 fresh rosemary sprig, leaves removed from stem and coarsely chopped

coarsely ground black pepper, to taste

honey, for drizzling

flaky sea salt, to taste

BLUE CHEESE FIG CRACKERS
1 (4.2-ounce) package oat crackers

½ cup fig jam

4 ounces Saint Agur blue or blue cheese of your liking

White Angel, Manhattan, Mississippi punch, or any champagne cocktail of your choice, to serve

THE BOARD
Place the canapés, Goat Cheese Apricot Crisps, and Blue Cheese Fig Crackers on a platter, keeping it super easy and casual. Serve from cocktail napkins instead of appetizer plates.

GOAT CHEESE APRICOT CRISPS
To assemble these sweet, fresh, and slightly tart goat cheese apricot crisps, spread about 1 teaspoon goat cheese on a cracker and top with an apricot slice. Repeat for the remaining crackers, and place on a plate. Sprinkle with rosemary and black pepper, drizzle with honey, and finish with flaky sea salt.

BLUE CHEESE FIG CRACKERS
To assemble these creamy, earthy, peppery, and sweet blue cheese fig crackers, spread each cracker with about 1 teaspoon of jam, flake off about a teaspoon of blue cheese, and place over the jam.

TIP: *As they did in the movie, serve the drinks in a mix of whatever you've got: paper cups, highballs, mugs, all of the above, whatever.*

You don't have to be named Bella to enjoy this Italian-inspired board. Fans of both the books and movies will enjoy the apple and flower imagery we know and love so well from the series. This selection of apples, dark chocolate, crostini, and biscotti paired with gorgonzola and salami is sure to bring the whole pack together and make your friends exclaim, "You brought a snack!"

Serves 4

THE BOARD

1 Rome or Macintosh apple

1 Fuji, Honeycrisp, or Pink Lady apple

6 ounces gorgonzola cheese

Mixed Berry Baked Brie Bites (see page 20)

Charcuterie Rosettes (see page 21)

¼ cup honey

8 Mulino Bianco Cioccograno cookies or other Italian cookies of your choice

2 cups mini biscotti, preferably with dried red fruit and nuts

1 handful of assorted breadsticks or crackers

3 ounces dark or semisweet chocolate bar, coarsely broken into medium to large pieces

½ cup Marcona almonds

3 tablespoons pomegranate arils

Homemade Crostini (see page 21)

pomegranate juice or a nice barolo, to serve

THE BOARD

Place the Rome or Macintosh apple in the center of the board. If the apple rolls or tilts to one side, slice off the bottom to create a stable base.

Halve the Fuji, Honeycrisp, or Pink Lady apple, remove the core, and cut each half into ¼-inch-thick slices. Carefully transport each half of the apple, making sure the slices maintain their original shape, and place them on opposite sides of the board. Place the gorgonzola in another open section of the board. Group the Mixed Berry Baked Brie Bites in opposite open sections of the board and do the same for the Charcuterie Rosettes, and add a jar or bowl of honey. Fill in the remaining open sections with cookies, biscotti, breadsticks or crackers, and chocolate bar sections. Add almonds to any last open areas, and lightly scatter pomegranate arils over the board. Arrange the crostini on a separate platter.

Serve with snack plates, a utensil assortment for the cheese and meat, and your beverage of choice.

MIXED BERRY BAKED BRIE BITES

1 sheet puff pastry, thawed according to package directions

8 ounces brie

¼ cup mixed berry jam

¼ cup chopped pecans (optional)

flaky sea salt, to taste

MIXED BERRY BAKED BRIE BITES

To make these mini baked brie bites with mixed berry jam, which are a nod to the berry cobbler Charlie Swan eats every week, preheat the oven to the temperature suggested on the package of puff pastry. Lightly spray a mini 24-cup muffin pan with nonstick cooking spray, and set aside.

Gently unroll the thawed puff pastry onto a lightly floured surface. Using a rolling pin, roll into an even shape, then cut the sheet lengthwise into 4 even strips and crosswise into 6 even strips. Each of the 24 squares will be about 2½ inches on each side. Gently separate the squares and press them into the mini muffin pan to create puff pastry cups, leaving the corners pointing upward. With the tines of a fork, prick the bottom of each puff pastry in 2 or 3 places.

Leaving the rind on, cut the brie into 1-inch cubes. Place 1 cube in each puff pastry cup, then add a small dollop, or ¼ teaspoon jam, over the brie, and top with a sprinkling of chopped pecans, if using.

Bake until the puff pastry is golden brown and crispy, about 12 minutes.

Let cool for 5 minutes before adding a sprinkling of flaky sea salt. Carefully remove the mini bites from the muffin pan while still warm to prevent sticking. Makes 24 brie bites.

TIP: *The mini bites are best made fresh and served warm. However, they can be assembled the night before and left in the fridge until ready to bake.*

CHARCUTERIE ROSETTES

4 ounces salami of your liking, very thinly sliced

HOMEMADE CROSTINI

½ baguette or demi baguette, sliced about ⅜ inch thick

2 tablespoons extra-virgin olive oil

½ teaspoon garlic powder (optional)

fine sea salt, to taste

CHARCUTERIE ROSETTES

Fold a slice of salami over the opening of a glass with a small mouth, like a champagne flute or a shot glass, making sure that half of the slice hugs the inside of the glass and half the outside.

Take the next slice, fold it, and place it halfway over the previous layer, again being careful that half of the slice is inside the glass and half outside. Press and mold the layers together with your fingers to keep the shape. The more layers you add, the fuller your rose will be.

Flip over the glass and remove the rosette so that the layered parts sitting inside the glass now face up. Gently mold the layered slices into a round shape if needed, and your rosette is complete. Repeat the process to make the second rosette.

HOMEMADE CROSTINI

Preheat the oven to 375°F. Line a baking sheet with foil or parchment paper.

Brush both sides of the baguette slices with olive oil and place on the baking sheet. Sprinkle the slices evenly with garlic powder, if using.

Bake until golden brown, about 7 minutes. Sprinkle with fine sea salt while warm.

You may not be able to catch that much-needed flight outta here, but you'll always have Paris...especially with this recipe for a straight French 75, a great drink to drown your troubles. Imagine yourself in the smoky lounge of Rick's Café Américain enjoying this Moroccan-style trail mix and roasted carrot and ricotta dip. Play (the movie) again and again, Sam.

Serves 2

THE BOARD
Mélange de Café Américain

Carottes de Résistance (see page 24)

6 ounces pita crackers

French 75, to serve (see page 24)

MÉLANGE DE CAFÉ AMÉRICAIN
1 (15-ounce) can garbanzo beans, rinsed, drained, and dried

1 tablespoon extra-virgin olive oil

1 teaspoon smoked paprika

½ teaspoon cinnamon

¼ teaspoon cumin

¼ teaspoon turmeric

⅛ teaspoon ginger powder

1 pinch cayenne

½ teaspoon kosher salt, plus more to taste

⅓ cup roughly chopped dried apricots

⅓ cup dried cherries

¼ cup shelled, roasted, and salted pistachios

½ cup whole roasted and salted almonds

THE BOARD
Serve a small bowl of the Mélange de Café Américain alongside the dip and crackers. Enjoy with a French 75.

MÉLANGE DE CAFÉ AMÉRICAIN
Preheat the oven to 375°F. Line a baking sheet with parchment paper, and set aside.

In a medium bowl, toss the garbanzo beans with the olive oil, spices, and salt. Place on the baking sheet. Bake for 10 minutes, toss, and bake for about 10 minutes more, until the garbanzo beans are crispy. Add extra salt to taste, and set aside to cool.

Add the crispy garbanzo beans, apricots, cherries, pistachios, and almonds to a large serving bowl, and toss to combine.

CAROTTES DE RÉSISTANCE

3 medium carrots, roughly chopped

3 teaspoons extra-virgin olive oil, divided, plus more for drizzling

½ teaspoon kosher salt, divided, plus more to taste

freshly ground black pepper

1 cup whole milk ricotta, drained

zest of ½ lemon

1 teaspoon tahini

¼ cup roughly chopped pistachios

FRENCH 75

2 ounces gin

½ ounce lemon juice

½ teaspoon simple syrup

chilled champagne

1 lemon twist

CAROTTES DE RÉSISTANCE

Preheat the oven to 425°F, and line a baking sheet with parchment paper or foil. Add the carrots, 2 teaspoon olive oil, ¼ teaspoon salt, and pepper, and toss to combine. Bake until fork tender with crispy edges, about 20 minutes, tossing the carrots halfway through.

Once the carrots have cooled, add them to the food processor, along with the ricotta, lemon zest, tahini, ¼ teaspoon salt, and 1 teaspoon olive oil. Puree until fully combined and fluffy. Add extra salt to taste. Place in a serving bowl, drizzle with olive oil, and sprinkle with the chopped pistachios.

TIP: *The dip can be made the night before (without any toppings) and stored in an airtight container.*

FRENCH 75

To a working glass with crushed ice, add the gin, lemon juice, and simple syrup, and stir to combine. Strain into a coupe or a collins glass with ice, add a champagne floater, and serve with a lemon twist.

IT'S CROQUE-ICATED
It's Complicated (2009)

You don't need to have trained in Paris to pull off this croque monsieur. But chocolate croissants are a bit trickier, as they aren't everyone's specialty. Better to pick up these buttery treats from a Meryl-approved bakery when you build this board. Packed with sweet and savory delights, the board will keep you satisfied as you watch this classic (and mouthwatering) Nancy Meyers film. If you know your rom-com tropes, you'll know it's best to stay away from toxic exes and perhaps keep your heart open to charming architects as you dig in.

Serves 4

THE BOARD

4 chocolate croissants, from your favorite French bakery or frozen

1 (6.25-ounce) package assorted mini quiches, baked according to package directions

Croque Monsieur (see page 27)

green salad

⅓ cup cornichons

crisp sauvignon blanc, to serve

THE BOARD

On a large platter, place the croissants and mini quiches. Cut the sandwiches in half, and place them with the salad on a separate large platter. Serve alongside a bowl of cornichons and glasses of cold, crisp white wine.

CROQUE MONSIEUR

2 tablespoons butter, plus more for brushing

2 tablespoons flour

2 cups whole milk

pinch of ground nutmeg

salt, to taste

freshly ground black pepper, to taste

8 slices country white bread

2 tablespoons Dijon or whole grain mustard

8 ounces thinly sliced black forest ham

8 ounces grated gruyère cheese, divided

CROQUE MONSIEUR

To make a béchamel sauce for the Croque Monsieur, melt the butter in a small saucepan over medium heat until foamy. Add the flour, stirring for 1 minute, then slowly whisk in the milk. Increase the heat to medium-high and boil until the sauce thickens, whisking constantly, about 2 minutes. Add the nutmeg, and season with salt and pepper to taste.

Preheat the broiler to low.

Place 4 slices of the bread on a work surface. Spread each lightly with mustard, and top each with a quarter of the ham. Set aside ½ cup of the grated cheese and add a quarter of the remaining cheese to each of the 4 bread slices. Top with the remaining 4 slices of bread.

Heat a large skillet over low heat. Brush both sides of the sandwiches with melted butter. Add them to the skillet and cook until golden brown, about 2 minutes per side. Transfer to a small baking sheet. Spoon the béchamel sauce and reserved grated cheese over the sandwiches, and sprinkle with black pepper to taste.

Broil until the cheese begins to get brown and bubbly, about 2 minutes. Serve immediately.

"A WOLF WITHOUT A FONDUE!"
Moonstruck (1987)

No need to bring out the big knife for this cheese pairing. This fondue nods at the iconic movie poster and pays homage to Cher's Oscar-winning performance as Loretta Castorini and her Italian-American heritage with a cacio e pepe–infused dip. You'll be absolutely moonstruck when you fall for this full moon/full bowl of cheese. Just make sure to snap out of it when slicing the bread, you don't want to lose a hand.

Serves 4

THE BOARD
Cacio e Pepe Fondue

1 loaf ciabatta or crusty bread of your choice, torn or cut into 1-inch chunks

Peroni or beer of your choice, to serve

CACIO E PEPE FONDUE
½ cup dry white wine, such as sauvignon blanc

1 tablespoon lemon juice

1 tablespoon cornstarch

6 ounces emmentaler, grated

6 ounces gruyère, grated

¾ cup pecorino romano, finely grated

½ tablespoon freshly ground black pepper, plus extra to taste

2 ounces gorgonzola

salt, to taste

THE BOARD
Serve this Swiss classic with an Italian twist in a fondue set or a heavy bowl, along with chunks of bread. Pair it with beer.

TIP: *When tearing or cutting the bread into chunks, retain as much of the crust as possible, as it adds stability when the bread is dipped in the fondue.*

CACIO E PEPE FONDUE
Place a large heatproof bowl over a pot of simmering water, and add the wine and lemon juice. Heat until steaming, then whisk in the cornstarch.

Adjust the heat to medium. In batches of thirds, add the emmentaler, gruyère, and pecorino romano, constantly stirring until each batch has melted. Add the black pepper and gorgonzola, whisking in long, folding movements until the fondue is fully combined and smooth. Add salt or extra pepper to taste. Keep the fondue warm over low heat until ready to serve.

"YOU HAVE BRIE-WITCHED ME, BODY AND SOUL"

Pride and Prejudice (2005)

This board filled with goodies inspired by Regency-era teatime speaks to Jane Austen's beloved classic and the 2005 film adaptation. Though the shades of Pemberley might be thus polluted if one were to bring this board to Lady Catherine, it is perfectly tolerable enough to share with one's friends and perhaps a tall, dark stranger with a quizzical brow (once he overcomes the inferiority of your birth, of course).

Serves 4

THE BOARD

assorted tea sandwiches (on this page and page 32)

⅓ cup clotted cream or whipped butter

4 personal-size jars assorted jams

6 mini or 4 full-size assorted scones (freshly baked or purchased from a local bakery)

½ pound assorted shortbread cookies and biscuits, such as Walkers

½ to 1 pound assorted dried or fresh fruit, such as apricots and cherries

tea, such as English Afternoon, along with milk, honey, or sugar, to serve

EGG SALAD TEA SANDWICHES

2 hard-boiled eggs

1 tablespoon mayonnaise

½ teaspoon Coleman's mustard (following package directions to make a paste) or Dijon mustard

½ teaspoon chopped fresh chives

salt, to taste

finely ground black pepper, to taste

4 slices thinly sliced white bread

THE BOARD

On a large serving platter or tiered dessert stand, arrange the sandwiches by type so that the contents are readily visible. Add the clotted cream or whipped butter and containers of jam, then fill large open spots with the scones and cookies and biscuits. Add the fruit to any remaining open spots. Serve with dessert plates, utensils, tea, and tea accoutrements.

EGG SALAD TEA SANDWICHES

Remove the yolks from the hard-boiled eggs and place them in a medium bowl. Add the mayonnaise and mustard, and mash to combine. Finely mince the egg whites, and add them to the bowl with the yolk mixture. Gently fold in the egg whites and chives to combine. Add salt and pepper to taste.

Add half of the egg salad to one slice of bread, and the other half to another slice of bread. Top each with a slice. Remove the crusts and cut in half crosswise to make triangles.

TIP: *The egg salad can be made a day ahead and stored in an airtight container in the fridge.*

CUCUMBER TEA SANDWICHES WITH CHIVE BUTTER

2 tablespoons salted butter, softened

½ teaspoon finely chopped chives

4 slices thinly sliced white bread

½ English cucumber, sliced ⅛ inch thick

BRIE, APPLE, AND PROSCIUTTO TEA SANDWICHES

1 tablespoon salted butter, softened

4 slices thinly sliced pumpernickel

1 tablespoon fig jam or preserves of your choice

4 ounces brie, cut into ⅛-inch slices

½ Granny Smith apple, thinly sliced and blotted to remove moisture

2 slices prosciutto

CREAM CHEESE AND SMOKED SALMON TEA SANDWICHES

2 tablespoons cream cheese, softened

4 slices thinly sliced pumpernickel

4 ounces smoked salmon, thinly sliced

2 tablespoons roughly chopped fresh dill

CUCUMBER TEA SANDWICHES

In a small bowl, mix the butter and chives to combine. Set aside.

Spread a thin layer of chive butter on one side of each slice of bread, crust to crust. Shingle cucumber slices onto one side of each sandwich, approximately 9 slices. Top with the other slice of bread. Gently pressing down to make sure each sandwich is secure, remove the crusts and cut each sandwich lengthwise into thirds, wiping off the knife between cuts. Serve immediately.

BRIE, APPLE, AND PROSCIUTTO TEA SANDWICHES

Spread a thin layer of butter on the inside of the bottom slices of bread, crust to crust. Spread a thin layer of jam or other preserves on the inside of the top slices of bread, crust to crust, and set aside. Place approximately 3 brie slices on each bottom slice. Layer on the apple slices, drape prosciutto slices on top, then cover with the top slices of bread. Gently press down to make sure each sandwich is secure, remove the crusts, and cut the sandwich lengthwise into thirds, wiping off the knife between cuts. Serve immediately.

CREAM CHEESE AND SMOKED SALMON TEA SANDWICHES

Spread a thin layer of cream cheese over each slice of bread, crust to crust. Gently place the smoked salmon onto each slice, crust to crust. Using a biscuit cutter or a fine-rimmed wine glass, cut the sandwich into a circle. Top with a pinch of fresh dill and serve immediately.

TIP: *Placing bread in the freezer for approximately an hour, if time allows, makes for a cleaner cut.*

"I'LL HAVARTI WHAT SHE'S HAVING"
When Harry Met Sally (1989)

This board is no consolation prize, Harry. It's honoring the iconic 1989 Nora Ephron rom-com that addresses whether straight men and women can ever be just friends. While Sally may take an hour and a half to order a *very satisfying* sandwich (with sauce on the side!), this NYC deli–inspired board is not high maintenance thinking it's low maintenance—the worst kind. It's quite easy to assemble. You make this board because when you realize you want to eat a pastrami sandwich, you want that meal to start as soon as possible.

Serves 4

THE BOARD

8 slices rye bread

1 pound pastrami

1 pound corned beef

8 ounces havarti with dill, cut into slices ¼ inch thick, then cut crosswise to make triangles

Mini Potato Knishes (see page 35)

12 mini hot dogs, cooked according to package directions

½ pound kosher dill pickles

¾ cup sauerkraut

½ pound coleslaw

⅓ cup spicy brown mustard

⅓ cup Russian dressing

THE BOARD

On a large board or serving tray (butcher block works well to emulate Katz's vibes), arrange the bread and meat. Lay out the havarti triangles, and scatter groupings of the knishes, hot dogs, and pickles. Then add small saucers of the sauerkraut, coleslaw, mustard, and Russian dressing.

Assemble the pastrami and corned beef into 2 sandwiches each, and don't forget to slather on condiments and pile on anything you like from the board. Slice each sandwich in half.

Serve with plates, forks, and utensils for the condiments.

MINI POTATO KNISHES

2 large russet potatoes, peeled and cut into large chunks

1 tablespoon extra-virgin olive oil

1 medium yellow onion, diced

1½ teaspoons kosher salt, divided, plus more to salt the water

freshly ground black pepper, to taste

¼ cup flour, for dusting

1 sheet puff pastry, thawed according to package directions

1 large egg, beaten

3 tablespoons sesame seeds

MINI POTATO KNISHES

In a medium saucepan, bring a full pot of water to a boil and season generously with kosher salt. Add the potatoes and boil until fork tender, approximately 20 minutes.

Meanwhile, warm the oil in a nonstick frying pan over medium-low heat until it shimmers. Add the onion and ½ teaspoon salt, and sauté low and slow. Stir constantly until the onions are deeply brown and caramelized, about 30 minutes. Remove from the stove to cool.

Drain the potatoes in a colander, and set aside to cool.

Preheat the oven to the temperature listed on the package of puff pastry. Line a baking sheet with parchment paper, and set aside.

Once the potatoes have cooled, add them to a medium bowl. Mash with a fork, leaving some small lumps for texture. Once the onion has cooled, add it to the bowl, along with 1 teaspoon of salt and freshly ground pepper to your liking, and combine.

Dust a clean work surface with flour. Gently unroll the thawed puff pastry over the dusted surface, and lightly use a rolling pin to even out the shape. Cut the longest side into 4 equal strips, then cut crosswise into 3 equal strips (4 strips if your puff pastry is more square than rectangular).

Fill each piece of puff pastry by adding 1 tablespoon of the potato mixture to the center. Pick up all four corners to wrap around the potato mixture, and pinch and twist the corners over the center to securely close the pastry. Repeat the process until all the pieces are filled and wrapped. Place the knishes on the lined baking sheet, spacing them approximately 2 inches apart. Brush the knishes with the beaten egg and sprinkle with the sesame seeds.

Bake until golden brown and puffed, 15 to 20 minutes. Serve warm. Makes 12 knishes.

TIP: *The mini potato knishes can be preassembled and frozen raw to be baked at a later date.*

KIDS EAT BRIE

KIDS' MOVIES AND MUSICALS

MY NEIGHBOR BENTO-TORO
Studio Ghibli (1985–present)

A new adventure awaits! There's no telling what it might entail, so why not pack your bento for every occasion? Pillowy red bean buns after a long day at the bathhouse, crispy gyoza for a romp through the market, wasabi peas hotter than a blazing demon, edamame to share with your furry neighbors, and an assemblage of your favorite Pocky flavors! What could be a more magical combination than that?

Serves 4

4 sweet red bean buns, cooked according to package directions

16 ounces gyoza, the type of your choice, cooked according to package directions

1 cup wasabi peas

14 ounces edamame in the shell, cooked according to package directions

2 or 3 boxes Pocky, assorted flavors

2 tablespoons soy sauce or dumpling dipping sauce

flaky sea salt, for sprinkling on edamame (optional)

Serve in bento boxes or on assorted small serving plates.

Somewhere over the rainbow, cheeseboards lie; there's a land that I dreamt of once in *Once Upon a Rind*! This *Wizard of Oz*–inspired cheeseboard has you following the yellow brick road straight to Oz. The beautiful rainbow spread will leave your guests jumping for joy, with Emerald City in sight during the first bite. Don't forget to slip on your ruby red slippers, and remember we aren't in Kansas anymore!

Serves 2

1 pint raspberries

1 cup red gummy bears or red candy of your choice

2 mandarins, peeled and sectioned

1 (4-ounce) block sharp cheddar, sliced ¼ inch thick, then cut into 1-inch-long bricks

1 cup green gummy bears, or green candy or vegetable of your choice

1 pint blueberries

1 cup purple gumdrops or purple candy of your choice

4 ounces honey blueberry chèvre, halved lengthwise and cut into ½-inch-thick slices

handful of crackers of your choice

On a large platter or plate, arrange the raspberries, red gummy bears, and mandarins in strips to begin forming the rainbow. Arrange the cheddar bricks in a staggered pattern to resemble the yellow brick road. Add strips of the green gummy bears, blueberries, purple gumdrops, and chèvre. Serve with a side of crackers, and you'll definitely say, "There's no place like home."

TIP: *If you can't track down any honey blueberry chèvre, try mixing spreadable goat cheese and blueberry jam instead!*

WILLY WONKA AND THE CHEESECAKE FACTORY

Willy Wonka and the Chocolate Factory (1971)

Oompah, loompah, doopity doo! I've got another snack board for you! Oompah, loompah, doopity dah! If you are wise you'll follow these steps! What should you do when friends are at your door? Serve a dessert that's perfect for four! How do you know what you should make? How about a simple no-bake cheesecake! Chopping into cubes will do the trick for this assortment of treats. Gummy candy and chocolates will take you far, if you need more sweets!

Serves 4

THE BOARD

Wonkalicious Cheesecake Bites (see page 44)

4 assorted rainbow lollipops

1 cup gumdrops in assorted colors

1 (1.77-ounce) package Everlasting Gobstoppers

1 cup gummy bears

1 (1.5-ounce) package candy buttons

1 (4.5-ounce) package Airheads Xtremes Rainbow Berry candy strips

12 Pixy Stix

1 cup M&M's

1 cup Sour Patch Kids

1 (3.1-ounce) package Sno-Caps

1 (5-ounce) package Mike and Ike

THE BOARD

Arrange the candy any which way you like on a large platter or in assorted glass jars and bowls. Serve the cheesecake bites on a separate dish.

WONKALICIOUS CHEESECAKE BITES

1 plain New York–style cheesecake, fresh or frozen

16 ounces semisweet chocolate chips

assorted sprinkles

16 lollipop sticks

WONKALICIOUS CHEESECAKE BITES

Line a baking sheet with parchment paper, and set aside. If using frozen cheesecake, follow the thawing directions on the package to thaw halfway. If using a fresh cheesecake, freeze for about 1 hour to firm up.

Once the cheesecake is firm, cut away the rounded edges so the cake is perfectly square. You can save discarded bits for another use or a chef's treat. Now cut the cake into 1-inch cubes, insert a lollipop stick into the center of each cube, and place on the baking sheet. Once all bites are on the sheet, put in the freezer for about 30 to 45 minutes.

Melt the chocolate chips in a bowl over a pot of simmering water or in the microwave. If using the microwave, melt and stir in 1-minute increments. Dip the firm cheesecake bites into the melted chocolate, letting any excess chocolate drip off, and place back on the baking sheet. Cover the bites with sprinkles while the chocolate is still gooey. Put the baking sheet back in the fridge to let the chocolate harden, about 1 hour. Makes about 16.

TIP: *Although fresh or frozen cheesecake can be used for this recipe, frozen works better.*

TIP: *The cheesecake bites can be made the night before and stored in an airtight container in the fridge.*

"THERE'S NO CRYING IN MOZZ-BALL"

A League of Their Own (1992)

When the boys are away, it's time for ladies to play ball! Buy yourself some peanuts and Cracker Jacks to enjoy this baseball-themed snack board complete with mini mozzarella baseballs. Take yourself out to the couch and cheer on the Rockford Peaches!

Serves 4

8 ounces mini mozzarella balls

2 tablespoons extra-virgin olive oil

pinch of salt

pinch of red pepper flakes

4 soft pretzels, heated according to package directions

4 cups roasted peanuts in the shell

4 (1-ounce) package Cracker Jack

12 mini corn dogs, cooked according to package directions

¼ cup ketchup

¼ cup yellow mustard

In a medium bowl, toss the mini mozzarella balls with the olive oil and the salt and red pepper flakes. Place in a small serving bowl.

Add the soft pretzels to one section of the board. Then add one half of the peanuts to another open section, and the other half to the opposite section. Add the bowl of mozzarella balls to an open area and cluster the Cracker Jack in another open area. Group the corn dogs, along ramekins of ketchup and mustard, in the last large open area.

Serve with snack plates and toothpicks.

When the Hogwarts Express trolley comes along, it's hard not to say, "We'll take the lot!" This board includes a sampling of all the delectable, magical treats offered on the scarlet steam engine, including chocolate frogs (good to have when there are dementors aboard), pumpkin pasties, and Harry's favorite, treacle tarts.

Serves 6

THE BOARD
Pumpkin Pasties

Treacle Tarts (see page 50)

½ pound English toffee

1 cup Bertie Bott's Beans or any assorted jelly beans

handful of Gringotts Galleon or any milk chocolate gold coins

1 cup Jelly Slugs or gummy worms

6 chocolate frogs

PUMPKIN PASTIES
Filling
1 cup canned pumpkin puree

1 Granny Smith apple, minced

¼ cup granulated sugar

⅛ teaspoon kosher salt

pinch of ground nutmeg

pinch of ground cinnamon

pinch of ground ginger

THE BOARD
On a large platter, place the Pumpkin Pasties, Treacle Tarts, and English toffee. Place the Bertie Bott's Beans or jelly beans in a small bowl, and add to the board. Fill in any open spaces with the gold coins, jelly slugs or gummy worms, and chocolate frogs.

PUMPKIN PASTIES
Combine all the filling ingredients in a medium bowl, mixing well until thoroughly incorporated.

To make the crust, put the flour, sugar, and salt into a food processor bowl, and pulse several times to combine. Scatter the chunks of butter and shortening over the flour mixture and pulse several times until everything is combined and resembles a coarse meal. No powdery bits should remain.

Transfer the mixture to a large bowl. Sprinkle 4 tablespoons of ice water over the mixture and mix with a spatula until it starts to clump together. If the mixture is too dry, add 1 tablespoon of ice water at a time until the texture is smooth.

Gather the dough into a ball and pat it into a disk shape. Wrap the disk in plastic wrap and chill in the refrigerator for 1 hour.

Pastry Crust
1¼ cups flour

1 tablespoon granulated sugar

¼ teaspoon salt

5 tablespoons cold butter, cut into chunks

3 tablespoons vegetable shortening, chilled and cut into chunks

4 to 6 tablespoons ice water

1 large egg, room temperature

1 tablespoon water

TREACLE TARTS
unsalted butter, for greasing

1¼ cups flour

1 tablespoon granulated sugar

¼ teaspoon salt

5 tablespoons cold butter, cut into chunks

3 tablespoons vegetable shortening, chilled and cut into chunks

4 to 6 tablespoons ice water, or more if needed

1 cup honey

¼ cup heavy cream

1 cup fresh breadcrumbs

zest and juice of 1 lemon

After the dough has chilled, preheat the oven to 400°F.

In a small bowl, whisk the egg and 1 tablespoon of water to make the egg wash. Set aside.

Roll the chilled dough to ⅛-inch thickness. Using a saucer, small plate, or bowl, cut out 6-inch circles. Place 1 to 2 teaspoons of filling in the center of each circle, and fold the dough over into a half circle. Moisten the edges of each circle with ice water and crimp with a fork to seal. Brush the top with the egg wash and cut small lightning bolt–shaped slits in the top of each pasty, to make vents that resemble Harry's scar.

Bake the pasties on an ungreased baking sheet until browned, about 30 minutes. Makes 6 pasties.

NOTE: *The recipe for Pumpkin Pasties was adapted from* The Unofficial Hogwarts for the Holidays Cookbook *by Rita Mock-Pike.*

TREACLE TARTS
Lightly grease the cups of a muffin pan with butter, and set aside.

Add the flour, sugar, and salt to the bowl of a food processor, and pulse a few times to combine. Scatter the butter and shortening over the flour mixture, and pulse several times until the mixture resembles a coarse meal. There should be no powdery residue left.

Transfer the mixture to a large bowl. Sprinkle 4 to 6 tablespoons of cold water over the mixture, and mix with a spatula until the dough begins to clump together. If it's too dry, add more water, 1 tablespoon at a time. It's better for the dough to be a little too wet than too dry.

Gather the dough into a ball. Wrap it in plastic wrap and refrigerate for 1 hour.

After the dough has chilled, preheat the oven to 375°F.

Remove the chilled dough from the fridge and punch to soften it into a moldable texture. If the dough is sticky, add 1 tablespoon of flour. If it is dry, add 1 tablespoon of ice water.

Roll the dough out, and use a glass or jar with a large enough mouth to cut out 12 disks large enough to line the bottoms and sides of the muffin cups.

Mix together the honey, heavy cream, breadcrumbs, lemon zest, and lemon juice in a medium bowl. Once the filling is thoroughly mixed, pour it into the crusts and bake the tarts until the filling is set, 30 to 40 minutes.

Remove from the oven and let cool for 5 minutes before serving. Makes 12 tarts.

NOTE: *The recipe for Treacle Tarts was adapted from* The Unofficial Hogwarts for the Holidays Cookbook *by Rita Mock-Pike.*

"KEEP THE CHEDDAR, YA FILTHY ANIMAL"
Home Alone (1990)

Since its release in 1990, *Home Alone* has become a family Christmas classic, known for its quotable phrases, hilarious high jinks, brilliant cast of actors, and touching ending. Get into the holiday spirit with this highly nutritious pizza and microwavable mac and cheese dinner fit for the man (or woman) of the house. As you prep the board, pop on the Kenosha Kickers "Polka, Polka, Polka," and don't forget the most important lesson—go easy on the Pepsi!

Serves 1

1 (10-ounce) personal-size pizza, microwaved according to package directions

1 (14-ounce) box mac and cheese, microwaved according to package directions

Keebler Rainbow Chips Deluxe Cookies, as many as you can possibly eat

large goblet of milk or Pepsi out of the can, to serve

Make sure the microwaved food is nice and warm, throw everything onto plates, and eat in front of the TV before you have to fight off the bad guys.

TIP: *This board's components can be homemade, but on an occasion like this, they just beg to be pulled out of the freezer and popped in the microwave.*

HOCUS PROSCIUTTO
Hocus Pocus (1993)

Hocus Pocus was a commercial flop turned cult classic that put a spell on '90s kids and adults alike. Whether you're spending a quiet evening at home or hosting a townful of youthful guests for dinner and a movie-viewing party, this snack board will fit all your needs. It includes a bit of everything—a little sweet, a little savory, everything but a dead man's toe. But don't feel the need to restrict yourself to the ingredients in this booooooooook—you can add anything, from newt's tail to the chocolate-covered finger of a man named Clark!

Serves 4

THE BOARD

4 ounces colby jack cheese, cut crosswise into ¼-inch slices

1 small celery stalk, cut into 1½-inch-long strips

6 mandarins, peeled

2 ounces prosciutto

½ cup Spanish olives with pimentos, or any green olives with pimentos

1 cup pumpkin cranberry crisps or crackers of your choice

1 cup pretzel crisps

1 cup gumdrops

½ cup Good & Plenty

1 cup Skittles

1 (3.25-ounce) package Pirouline chocolate hazelnut cookies

½ cup gummy worms

Child Skeleton Gingerbread Cookies and Other Creepy Creatures (see page 56)

Lime Rickey, to serve (see page 57)

THE BOARD
To assemble this spooky snack plate, begin by shingling the slices of colby jack to create a river of cheese through the board. Insert celery strips into mandarin tops to make pumpkin stems. Place the "pumpkins" on opposing corners of the board, drape a prosciutto mound, and add a bowl of olives with the pimentos facing up to resemble eyes.

Add the crackers and pretzel crisps, and fill the remaining spaces with gumdrops, Good & Plenty, and Skittles. Tuck Pirouline cookies in nooks around the perimeter, place gummy worms throughout the board so they appear to be crawling, set the spell book in a prime location, tuck the child skeleton gingerbread cookies around the board, and scatter the yogurt-covered pretzel ghouls and the chocolate-covered Oreos. And whatever you do, don't forget the lime rickeys.

CHILD SKELETON GINGERBREAD COOKIES AND OTHER CREEPY CREATURES

1½ cups milk chocolate or semisweet chocolate chips

1 graham cracker sheet

1 box candy eyes in assorted sizes

8 Oreo cookies

½ cup white chocolate chips

8 Pepperidge Farm Gingerman cookies

12 yogurt-covered pretzels

1 cup black candy melts

CHILD SKELETON GINGERBREAD COOKIES AND OTHER CREEPY CREATURES

Line 2 baking sheets with parchment paper, and set aside.

Melt the chocolate chips in a medium bowl set over a pot of simmering water or in the microwave. If using the microwave, melt and stir in 1-minute increments. To make the spell book, dip the graham cracker in the chocolate, letting any excess drip off, place on the baking sheet, and add one large eyeball. To make the chocolate-covered Oreos, dip the cookies in chocolate using the same technique, place on the baking sheet, and add 2 eyeballs each. Put in the fridge to harden, about 30 minutes.

To make the child skeleton cookies, melt the white chocolate chips in a small bowl using the same technique as for melting the chocolate chips. Place the Gingerman cookies on the baking sheet. Transfer the melted white chocolate to a small zip-top bag, and snip off the tip very close to the edge. Pipe the white chocolate on the cookies so they look like little skeletons, and add small eyeballs. Place in the fridge to harden, about 20 minutes.

To make the yogurt pretzel ghouls, place the yogurt-covered pretzels on the baking sheet. Melt the black candy melts in a small bowl in the microwave, then transfer to a small zip-top bag, and snip off the tip very close to the edge. Pipe the black candy melts into the top two pretzel holes, add two candy eyes, then place in the fridge to harden, about 20 minutes. Using the remaining melted black candy, pipe flourishes on the spell book. Place in the fridge to harden, about 15 minutes.

LIME RICKEY

8 ounces lime juice

4 ounces simple syrup

1 or 2 drops green food coloring (optional)

12 ounces seltzer water

4 ounces gin or vodka (optional)

lime slices, for garnish

LIME RICKEY

Mix the lime juice, simple syrup, and food coloring, if using, in a measuring cup. Fill 4 highball glasses with ice. Divide the lime and simple syrup mixture among the 4 glasses. Top off each glass with seltzer water, and garnish with a lime slice.

TIP: *To adultify the lime rickey, add 1 ounce of gin or vodka per drink.*

NOTE: *The recipe for Lime Rickey was inspired by the book XOXO, A Cocktail Book by Bridget Thoreson.*

"THE HILLS ARE OLIVE WITH THE SOUND OF MUSIC"

The Sound of Music (1965)

A favorite of nuns, governesses, and overwhelmed fathers tired of chasing after their errant children, this board features both savory bites and delicious Austrian sweets meant to keep the whole family fed, happy, and singing "Do-Re-Me." This picnic board will quickly become one of your favorite things, best enjoyed in a field or throughout this nearly three-hour classic (don't skimp on the stroopwafel!)

Serves 4

2 pounds assorted fresh fruit, such as pears and red grapes

1 apple strudel (about 1 pound)

4 ounces herbed chèvre

8 ounces brie

¼ cup mixed berry jam

¼ cup honey

⅓ cup Castelvetrano olives

4 slices brown bread, such as brown sourdough with fruit and nuts

handful of assorted cookies, such as mini stroopwafels and loackers

1 cup roasted and unsalted almonds

In a shallow but wide basket, group the fruit by type around the perimeter. Place the strudel in the center, and add the cheeses in opposite open areas. Begin filling in open spaces with containers of jam, honey, and olives. Halve the bread slices, and add them along with the cookies and almonds to fill in any gaps.

Serve with snack plates, cheese spreaders, and a honey dipper or spoon.

Curd morning, curd morning! This classic Hollywood-themed board brings all your favorite movie theater snacks together to watch the best movie about making movies. As Gene, Donald, and Debbie tap-dance through their iconic musical numbers, you can settle into the couch with your favorite candies (feel free to sub out for your favorites). What a glorious feeling, you'll be happy again in no time.

Serves 4

6 ounces Point Reyes original blue cheese or a mild blue cheese of your choice

4-ounce kunik or triple crème brie

4 ounces prosciutto

16 ounces strawberries

½ cup Marcona almonds

1 cup gummy bears

1 (3.5-ounce) package Junior Mints

1 (3.1-ounce) package Sno-Caps

1 cup M&M's

1 (7-ounce) package red Twizzlers

1 cup Sour Patch Kids

4 ounces olive oil and sea salt sourdough crackers or crackers of your choice

6 cups movie theater–style popcorn

On a large platter or board, place the cheeses in opposing sections. Carefully drape the prosciutto into cascading ribbons, and place the strawberries in a cluster. Then add groupings of the almonds, gummy bears, Junior Mints, Sno-Caps, M&M's, Twizzlers, and Sour Patch Kids. Place the crackers in any open spaces, and serve with a large bowl of popcorn.

A brie is a wish your heart makes, or in the case of this spread, a bunch of mini brie accompanied by some delicious snackery is a wish come true. This platter has a little something from every era of fairy tale, from the original *Snow White* to the more modern take of *Frozen*. But don't worry, there are no poisoned apples or enchanted roses here! Just snacks that will make you the happiest fan on earth.

Serves 4

THE BOARD

1 red apple, halved and sliced

Charcuterie Rosettes

4 mini brie

¼ cup red jam of your choice

1 cup mixed nuts

½ cup chocolate-covered raisins

Frozen Snowflake Cookies (see page 64)

4 ounces Pepperidge Farm Golden Butter crackers or buttery crackers of your choice

7 ounces crab dip

4 cupcakes, preferably with rose icing

tea, to serve

CHARCUTERIE ROSETTES

6 ounces salami of your liking, very thinly sliced

THE BOARD

On a platter, add the sliced apple, charcuterie roses, brie, and jam. Add clusters of the nuts and chocolate-covered raisins, and scatter the cookies and crackers around the rim. Place the crab dip in a small bowl, and position it and the cupcakes near the platter. Serve with cups of tea. And don't forget the dinglehopper!

CHARCUTERIE ROSETTES

Using the method described here, you should have enough salami to make 3 rosettes. Begin the first rosette by folding a salami slice in half and layering it over the opening of a glass with a small mouth, like a champagne flute or shot glass. Make sure that half of the slice hugs the inside of the glass and half the outside.

Take the next slice, fold it, and lay it halfway over the previous layer, again being careful that half of the slice is inside the glass and half outside. Press and mold the layers with your fingers to keep the shape. The more layers you add, the fuller your rose will be.

Flip over the glass and remove the rosette so that the layered parts sitting inside the glass now face up. Gently mold the layered slices into a round shape if needed, and your rosette is complete. Repeat the process for the other rosettes.

FROZEN SNOWFLAKE COOKIES

1 (16.5-ounce) tube sugar cookie dough

1 cup flour, plus extra for dusting

coarse silver sprinkling sugar

FROZEN SNOWFLAKE COOKIES

Preheat the oven to 350°F. Line a baking sheet with parchment paper, and set aside.

Dust a clean work surface with flour. Knead half the dough with half the flour, and roll out with a flour-dusted rolling pin, until ¼ inch thick. Using a flour-dusted cookie cutter in the shape of a snowflake, cut out the cookies and place on the sheet, about 2 inches apart. Sprinkle with sprinkling sugar, lightly pressing into the dough if needed. Repeat the process with the second batch of dough.

Bake until golden brown, about 7 to 9 minutes. Let sit on the baking sheet for 5 minutes, then move to a cooling rack to cool completely.

RITZ A WONDERFUL LIFE
It's a Wonderful Life (1946)

It's a Wonderful Life is mandatory viewing every holiday season. The film follows George Bailey (Jimmy Stewart) as he sees what life would be like if he'd never been born. It begs the question: what would happen if cheese was never invented? Our lives and Christmas would certainly be worse off without it. So gather your friends and family around this snack board to appreciate your blessings: loved ones and cheese. And remember: whenever a Baby*bell* rings an angel gets its wings.

Serves 2

THE BOARD
Charcuterie Rosettes (see page 66)

1 medium-size chocolate Santa or Christmas candy of your choice

1 bunch red grapes

2 ounces Secchi salami or any narrow dry Italian sausage, sliced into 1/16-inch rounds

2 ounces pecorino, flaked

3 Babybel cheeses

4 ounces Midnight Moon cheese or any semifirm cheese, sliced into 1/4-inch-thick triangles

handful of assorted crackers, such as raisin, rosemary, and pumpkin seed

handful of Ritz crackers or any cracker of your choice

8 shortbread cookies or any festive Christmas cookies

1/4 cup caramelized walnuts

1/4 cup pistachios

THE BOARD
On a round platter or large plate, lay out greenery or woody herbs around the perimeter, to create the base for a wreath. At the bottom center, place the larger charcuterie rosettes. Position the chocolate Santa or Christmas candy toward one side of the wreath. Begin to add small clusters of grapes, sausage, and pecorino throughout the wreath. Add the Babybels (leaving the red wax on for a festive look) and small charcuterie rosettes. In open spaces, fan out the slices of Midnight Moon or semifirm cheese, and place the crackers and cookies in clusters. Sprinkle the nuts over the wreath or stuff them into the remaining open nooks.

TIP: *Use assorted greenery or woody herbs, such as rosemary, for the wreath base.*

CHARCUTERIE ROSETTES

4 ounces salami of your liking, very thinly sliced, for 2 larger rosettes

2 ounces peppered Genoa salami or salami of your choice, very thinly sliced, for 2 or 3 small rosettes

CHARCUTERIE ROSETTES

To make the larger rosettes, use a glass with a small mouth, like a champagne flute or shot glass. Begin the first rosette by folding a salami slice in half and layering it over the opening of the glass. Make sure that half of the slice hugs the inside of the glass and half the outside.

Take the next slice, fold it, and layer it halfway over the previous layer, again being careful that half of the slice is inside the glass and half outside. Press and mold the layers with your fingers to keep the shape. The more layers you add, the fuller your rose will be.

Flip over the glass and remove the rosette so that the layered parts sitting inside the glass now face up. Gently mold the layered slices into a round shape if needed, and your rosette is complete. Repeat the process for the second rosette.

To make each of the small rosettes, lay 4 pieces of salami on a flat surface and overlap them an inch or two. Fold all 4 pieces together in half lengthwise. Starting from one side, tightly roll the folded pieces until they form a rose shape. Then push a toothpick through the rose to hold it together.

"IT'S A BOG OF ETERNAL STILTON!"
Labyrinth (1986)

Jim Henson's cult classic takes food form in this bewitching spread. From dates representing the actual dates Sarah's stepmother thought she should be going on (instead of playing in her fantasy world) to blue cheese representing the Bog of Eternal Stench, these snacks are sure to have your taste buds doing a magic dance in celebration of the Goblin King and the babe with the power.

Serves 4

THE BOARD
"Bog of Eternal Stilton" Stuffed Dates

Jareth's Mozzarella Balls

Prosciutto-Wrapped Peaches (see page 69)

8 peach macarons or peach cookies

champagne or prosecco, to serve

"BOG OF ETERNAL STILTON" STUFFED DATES
12 medjool dates

2 ounces stilton or any blue cheese of your choice

2 tablespoons slivered almonds

honey, for drizzling

flaky sea salt, for finishing

JARETH'S MOZZARELLA BALLS
8 ounces whole milk mini mozzarella balls

½ cup extra-virgin olive oil

½ teaspoon kosher salt

¼ teaspoon red pepper flakes

freshly ground black pepper, to taste

1 teaspoon chopped fresh parsley

1 clove garlic, smashed

2 slivers lemon rind

THE BOARD
Place the components on separate serving pieces or group them on one large platter or board. Serve alongside appetizer plates, utensils, and champagne or prosecco.

"BOG OF ETERNAL STILTON" STUFFED DATES
Preheat the broiler to low and line a baking sheet with parchment paper.

Gently slice open each date lengthwise, but not all the way through, and remove the pit. Stuff with the cheese, approximately 1 teaspoon per date, and place on the sheet. Broil until warm and slightly crisp on the edges, approximately 3 minutes.

Wait until the stuffed dates are on the serving piece to sprinkle the slivered almonds, lightly drizzle the honey, and finish with a sprinkle of flaky sea salt. Serve warm.

JARETH'S MOZZARELLA BALLS
Drain the mozzarella well, and set aside. In a medium bowl, combine the olive oil, salt, red pepper, black pepper, and parsley, and whisk to combine. Add the garlic, lemon rind, and mozzarella, folding gently to combine. Marinate in the fridge for about 1 hour before serving.

PROSCIUTTO-WRAPPED PEACHES

2 peaches

4 ounces prosciutto

1 tablespoon extra-virgin olive oil

balsamic reduction, for drizzling

flaky sea salt, to taste

PROSCIUTTO-WRAPPED PEACHES

Preheat the oven to 425°F and line a baking sheet with parchment paper.

Slice each peach in half and remove the pit, then cut each half into quarters. Cut the prosciutto slices in half and wrap each peach segment with a half prosciutto slice. Place on the sheet and lightly drizzle with olive oil.

Bake until warmed through, about 7 minutes. Then turn the broiler to low and broil until the edges are crisp, about 2 minutes.

Wait until placing the prosciutto-wrapped fruit on the serving piece to drizzle with the balsamic reduction and sprinkle with flaky sea salt. Serve warm. Makes 16.

NOTE: *The macarons shown here are by Juice Stand Macarons. Instagram @juicestandmacarons*

If you're lost on what to serve at your next Halloween party or role-playing gaming session or whatever, just remember: you have absolute power. These moist and fudgy peanut butter blondie bars—an updated take on the classic blondie—are sure to please anyone, from goblins and coyotes to spacemen and government agents. Pair with a nice refreshing glass of Coke.

Serves 4

THE BOARD

Reese's Pieces Peanut Butter Blondies (see page 72)

1 cup Reese's Pieces

Coke, to serve

THE BOARD

Place the blondies on a large serving plate, scatter the Reese's Pieces around the blondies, and serve with Coke.

REESE'S PIECES PEANUT BUTTER BLONDIES

2 cups flour

1 teaspoon baking soda

1½ teaspoons kosher salt

¾ cup unsalted butter

1½ cups packed brown sugar

1 tablespoon vanilla

2 large eggs, room temperature

¾ cup creamy salted conventional peanut butter, not natural

2 cups Reese's Pieces, divided

REESE'S PIECES PEANUT BUTTER BLONDIES

Preheat the oven to 375°F. Spray an 8 x 8-inch baking pan with cooking spray and line with parchment paper. Leave the ends of the paper long enough so they can be used to lift the blondies out of the pan once baked. Set aside.

In a medium bowl, combine the flour, baking soda, and salt, and set aside.

In a large bowl, add the butter, brown sugar, vanilla, and eggs. Using a mixer, beat until combined. Add the peanut butter, and beat until incorporated. In one-third increments, beat in the flour mixture until fully combined. Fold in all but 2 tablespoons of Reese's Pieces. Spread the mixture evenly into the baking pan and sprinkle the reserved Reese's Pieces on top of the batter.

Bake until an inserted toothpick comes out mostly dry with just a fine crumb, about 30 minutes. Let rest in the pan for 10 minutes, then finish cooling on a rack. Slice in thirds in both directions to make 9 large blondies, or cut into smaller pieces if desired.

TIP: *Blondies can be kept in a sealed container at room temperature for up to a week.*

IF BOARDS CURD KILL

ACTION AND DRAMA

FETA & FURIOUS
Fast & Furious (2001–present)

What's the best way to celebrate stealing DVD players, winning a Tokyo street race, stopping an international supervillain, or literally blasting a car into space? A good barbecue with your family (because nothing is more important than FAMILY). Put on your favorite white tank top, crack open an ice-cold Corona, grill up some cheese, and gather your crew to enjoy a snack board inspired by this wildly popular and epic film series. Don't forget to pour one out for our brother, Paul.

Serves 4

THE BOARD
Grilled Feta

6 ounces habanero cheddar cheese or cheddar jack, sliced ¼ inch thick

4 ounces assorted jerky

Mini Jalapeño Cheddar Cornbread (see page 76)

16 ounces slaw of your choice

1 (16-ounce) bag mesquite BBQ potato chips

½ cup cornichons or bread and butter pickles

½ cup Peppadew peppers

Corona and lime slices, to serve

GRILLED FETA
1 (8-ounce) block feta in brine, not crumbled

olive oil, for rubbing

kosher salt, for sprinkling

fresh herbs, such as thyme and parsley, for sprinkling

THE BOARD
On a large serving platter or board, add the grilled feta, cheddar cheese, and assorted jerky. Place the cornbread in a bowl or basket, and the slaw, cornichons or bread and butter pickles, and Peppadew peppers in individual small bowls. Scatter them on the platter or board. Serve with Corona and lime slices.

GRILLED FETA
Preheat the broiler to low. Line a baking sheet with aluminum foil.

Remove the feta from the brine and pat it dry with a paper towel or a clean dish towel. Slice the feta into 4 equal-size planks and place on the sheet. Gently rub both sides with olive oil, and sprinkle with salt and whatever herbs you are using. Broil until golden brown and warmed through, about 2 to 5 minutes.

Use a spatula to transfer the grilled feta to the serving platter or board. Wait until it's there before adding a drizzle of fresh olive oil and a sprinkle of herbs. Serve warm.

MINI JALAPEÑO CHEDDAR CORNBREAD

3 cups cornmeal

2 tablespoons baking powder

3 tablespoons sugar

1 teaspoon red pepper flakes

2½ teaspoons kosher salt

2 cups whole milk

½ cup canola oil

1 (14.25-ounce) can cream-style corn

8 ounces shredded sharp cheddar cheese, divided

1 (4-ounce) can fire-roasted green chiles

MINI JALAPEÑO CHEDDAR CORNBREAD

Preheat the oven to 375°F. Generously spray a mini muffin pan with nonstick spray, and set aside.

In a large bowl, combine the cornmeal, baking powder, sugar, red pepper flakes, and salt. Whisk until combined, taking care not to overmix. Add the milk, oil, and corn, and whisk until just combined. Set aside ½ cup of the shredded cheddar, then fold in the remaining cheddar and the chiles.

Fill each cup of the mini muffin pan to the rim with batter, about 1 tablespoon. Sprinkle the reserved cheddar cheese on top.

Bake until the edges are golden and an inserted toothpick comes out clean, about 15 minutes. Let rest for 10 minutes in the muffin pan, and then remove to a cooling rack to fully cool. Makes about 24 mini muffins.

"LIFE FINDS A WHEY"
Jurassic Park (1993)

Hold onto your butts, because this snack board is one for the ages. Create this scientist-approved board of cheese skewers, dino nuggets, dino fruit cutouts, and banana pudding cups, and you'll satiate the ravenous appetites of carnivores and herbivores alike. Be sure to spare no expense when gathering the ingredients. Expect to feed quite the team of adventurers.

Serves 4

CHEESE SKEWERS

1 (8-ounce) block mild yellow cheddar

1 (8-ounce) block sharp white cheddar

12 small skewers or toothpicks

DINO FRUIT CUTOUTS

1 pineapple

1 pint blueberries

2 kiwis, sliced into ¼-inch rounds

DINO NUGGETS

12 ounces dinosaur chicken nuggets, heated according to package directions

¼ cup each of barbecue sauce, honey mustard, and ketchup, for dipping

CHEESE SKEWERS

Cut the blocks of cheese into 1-inch cubes. Place two cubes on a skewer, staggering white and yellow cheeses. Place upright on a plate or platter. Makes 12 skewers.

DINO FRUIT CUTOUTS

Remove the crown and skin from the pineapple, and slice the flesh into ½-inch rounds. If using a cookie cutter, press into the flesh to create a dino or animal shape. If not using a cookie cutter, cut into quarters.

Arrange the fruit on a platter by scattering kiwi slices along the bottom and placing the dino or pineapple quarters on top. Scatter the blueberries in open spaces.

DINO NUGGETS

Place a larger bowl of the chicken nuggets and small bowls of dipping sauces on the platter near the dino fruit cutouts.

BANANA PUDDING CUPS

1 package heat-and-serve vanilla pudding

milk, if your vanilla pudding requires it

1 tub Cool Whip or refrigerated whipped topping of your choice, thawed

2 bananas

1 package Pepperidge Farm Chessmen or vanilla cookies of your choice

BANANA PUDDING CUPS

In a medium to large saucepan, cook the vanilla pudding according to package directions. Set aside to cool. Add the whipped topping to the pan with the cooled pudding, and whisk to combine.

Slice the bananas into ⅛-inch-thick rings.

In a large bowl or individual containers, assemble the banana pudding by placing 1 layer of the vanilla cookies on the bottom of the container, then adding a layer of banana pudding mixture, followed by a layer of banana slices. Repeat the process until the container is almost filled, finishing with a layer of the pudding mixture.

Place the remaining vanilla cookies in a zip-top bag. Use your hands to crush the cookies until they have a coarse and crumbly texture. Sprinkle the crushed cookies on top of the pudding so that they look like rocks. If desired, top the pudding with decorative miniature dinosaurs. Place the pudding cups in the fridge for 2 to 24 hours to soften the cookies. Makes about 12 pudding cups.

FIGHT CLUB (CRACKERS)
Fight Club (1999)

Go to your local corner store. Find the most generic snack brands. Now is not the time for the Starbucks venti mocha whatever, or for some experimental pastries from that new hipster spot your friends told you about. You are not Martha f*cking Stewart. The cheapest and fattiest donuts, cookies, and club cracker sandwiches you can find paired with the blackest of coffee is all you need to hit rock-bottom with your single-serving friends.

Serves 6

1 box assorted donuts

1 package chocolate chip cookies

1 package duplex sandwich cookies

1 package frosted oatmeal cookies

1 package shortbread cookies

1 package Keebler Club and Cheddar Sandwich Crackers

1 pot black coffee

assorted creamers and sweetener packets, to serve

Assemble the donuts, cookies, and crackers on a simple, no-frills platter. Serve with black coffee in paper cups along with individual creamers, packets of sugar, and stirrers for your single-serving friends.

Construct a droid-shaped ball of cheese you will, young padawan. Awaken the Force (or, in this case, the Fromage) within you and become the Jedi Master you were born to be as you create the cutest and tastiest cheese ball in the galaxy. Serving this board with a side of crunchy galactic mix easily makes this spread the best snack from here to the Outer Rim.

Serves 4

THE BOARD

BB-8 Cheese Ball (see page 84)

Galactic Mix (see page 85)

handful of assorted crackers

crudités, of your choice

THE BOARD

Place the assorted crudités and crackers on the serving plate with the BB-8 cheese ball. Position the galactic mix on its own serving plate, in a nearby orbit.

BB-8 CHEESE BALL

2 (8-ounce) packages cream cheese, softened

⅓ cup sour cream

2 green onions, white parts only, finely sliced

1½ teaspoons garlic powder

1 teaspoon onion powder

3 or 4 drops hot sauce

½ teaspoon finely ground black pepper

¼ teaspoon kosher salt

1 (8-ounce) block sharp white cheddar, finely shredded

¼ pound sliced yellow cheddar

1 black olive, cut in half

BB-8 CHEESE BALL

To a large bowl, add the cream cheese, sour cream, green onions, garlic powder, onion powder, hot sauce, pepper, and salt. Using a hand or stand mixer, beat on medium until fully combined. Add the shredded cheese, and use a rubber spatula to combine. Place in the fridge for 1 hour to firm up.

Spray your hands with nonstick cooking spray. Use three-quarters of the cheese mixture to form a round ball for BB-8's bottom. Spray your hands again if needed, and roll the remaining mixture into a ball, flattening the bottom on the counter or a plate, for BB-8's head. Place both balls in the freezer for about 30 minutes, to ensure they hold their shape.

Meanwhile, use a mat knife or a sharp paring knife on a cutting board to create 5 circles from the sliced yellow cheese for BB-8's body. It is helpful to use a cookie cutter, a biscuit cutter, or a small glass to cut the main circle. You can make a template for the center cutout or cut it freehand. Cut thin cheese strips for BB-8's head, and use the olive halves for his sensors/lenses.

Place the larger cheese ball in the center of a serving dish or platter. Use a wood skewer for support. Push it into the center of the larger ball and break off the excess, so that only 1½ to 2 inches stick out of the top. Place the smaller cheese ball over the skewer, pressing down gently. Add the cheese circles to the larger ball, and the cheese strips and sliced olives to the head.

TIP: *This cheese ball is best made a day in advance and kept in the fridge covered in plastic wrap. Make BB-8's decorations the day the cheese ball will be served, so they do not appear dried out.*

GALACTIC MIX

1 (12-ounce) bag red chocolate melts

1 (12-ounce) bag blue chocolate melts

20 pretzels sticks

¼ cup yogurt-covered raisins

½ cup chocolate-covered nuts or raisins

½ cup puffed cereal of your choice

¼ cup M&M's

2 tablespoons star sprinkles

1 tablespoon silver sprinkles

GALACTIC MIX

To make the lightsaber pretzels, line a baking sheet with parchment paper, and set it aside. Melt half the bag of red chocolate melts and half the bag of blue chocolate melts, following package directions. Save the unused melts for another project. Place the melted red chocolate in a small juice glass, and the melted blue chocolate in another small juice glass. Dip half the pretzels into the red chocolate about three-quarters of the way up the pretzel, letting any excess chocolate drip off. Place the dipped pretzels on the baking sheet to cool. Repeat the process for the blue chocolate. Put the lightsabers in the fridge for 15 to 20 minutes to fully harden.

In a medium bowl, add the yogurt-covered raisins, chocolate-covered raisins or nuts, cereal, and M&Ms, and toss to combine. Add the lightsaber pretzels, tossing gently to combine. Transfer the mixture to its own serving dish and top with the assorted sprinkles.

Put on your fedora, grab your bullwhip, and saddle up for an archeological adventure with Indy and this Middle Eastern mezze platter. This absolutely packed snack board will give you the energy to outrun a boulder, escape a temple, or marathon the original trilogy (Let's not talk about the fourth and future installments). These dates definitely aren't bad and there don't have to be snakes when you plate this one.

Serves 2

THE BOARD
Stuffed Medjool Dates

Baba Ghanoush (see page 88)

Grilled Halloumi (see page 88)

1 cup mixed olives

2 large lavash, or a handful of pita crackers

shots of whiskey, to serve

STUFFED MEDJOOL DATES
2 tablespoons tahini paste

¼ teaspoon vanilla extract

1 teaspoon honey, plus more for drizzling

squeeze of lemon juice

pinch of cinnamon

pinch of kosher salt

6 medjool dates

3 tablespoons chopped salted pistachios

THE BOARD
Place all items of this sweet and savory mezze platter—the stuffed dates, baba ghanoush, grilled Halloumi, and olives—on a serving plate, and serve with warm lavash or pita crackers. Accompany with shots of whiskey.

STUFFED MEDJOOL DATES
In a small bowl, combine the tahini, vanilla, honey, lemon juice, cinnamon, and salt, and stir to combine.

Slice the dates in half lengthwise, taking care not to cut all the way through, and remove the pits. Stuff each date with about 1 teaspoon of the pistachios, then drizzle the tahini mixture over the nuts.

Finely chop the remaining pistachios and sprinkle them over the stuffed dates. Drizzle with honey. Makes 6 stuffed dates.

TIP: *The dates can be stuffed a day ahead of time and kept on the counter in an airtight container. To keep the finely chopped pistachios crunchy, add them and the honey the day the dates will be served.*

BABA GHANOUSH

1 pound eggplant, preferably 2 smaller ones

2 tablespoons extra-virgin olive oil, plus extra for drizzling

2 tablespoons tahini paste

1 tablespoon plain yogurt (eliminate to keep dairy-free)

1 tablespoon lemon juice, plus extra to taste

1 clove garlic, grated

½ teaspoon sumac, plus extra for sprinkling

pinch of Aleppo pepper or cayenne

1 teaspoon kosher salt, plus extra to taste

1 tablespoon chopped parsley, for garnish (optional)

GRILLED HALLOUMI

8 ounces Halloumi

1 tablespoon extra-virgin olive oil

toppings, such as honey, toasted sesame seeds, blistered tomatoes, and olive oil (optional)

BABA GHANOUSH

Preheat the oven to 425°F and line a baking sheet with foil.

Rub the eggplant with olive oil. If you have a gas burner, hold the eggplant directly over the open flame with tongs, and char all sides until the fruit begins to shrivel and wilt. Place it on the sheet and bake until completely withered, about 15 to 20 minutes. If you don't have gas, place directly in the oven. Set aside the baked eggplant to cool.

Once the eggplant is completely cool, remove the skin and stem. Small pieces of charred skin are OK, as they add great flavor and texture. Place the eggplant in a colander, pushing down with a wooden spoon to release remaining liquids, while breaking the flesh into small pieces.

In a medium bowl, add the eggplant flesh, tahini, yogurt (if using), lemon juice, garlic, sumac, pepper, and salt. Mix to combine. Add any extra lemon juice or salt, to taste.

After transferring to a serving dish, top with a drizzle of extra virgin olive oil, a sprinkle of sumac, and parsley, if using. This recipe yields more than the board is meant to serve. Indulge in the excess now or save the rest for later!

GRILLED HALLOUMI

Cut the block of Halloumi in half lengthwise, and blot any excess moisture with a clean kitchen towel.

Heat a nonstick pan over medium heat. Add the olive oil, warming it until it shimmers. Add the Halloumi and cook until golden brown, about 5 minutes per side.

For a sweet option, drizzle with honey and toasted sesame seeds. For a savory option, top with blistered tomatoes and a drizzle of olive oil. Add salt to taste. Serve warm.

"BEANS. LOTS OF JELLY BEANS."

The Matrix (1999)

You're a bit like Alice right now: tumbling down the rabbit hole, searching for the greatest snack board you could ever serve. Something that's simple in presentation and easy to put together but also breathes nuance and complexity. And yet you have the look of someone who doesn't want to make a difficult choice. It's right on your face. But don't worry—you don't have to choose between the red and blue jelly beans. They both lead you to the same path, anyway.

10 ounces red jelly beans

10 ounces blue jelly beans

On a circular board or platter, line up the jelly beans vertically, alternating colors at random, so the pattern appears as digital code. Bend a spoon with your mind and enjoy.

"YOU'RE GONNA NEED A BIGGER GOAT (CHEESE)"

Jaws (1975)

Nothing keeps you out of the water like the pure terror of a great white shark (not a tiger shark), particularly one that has a ton of buildup but only around four minutes of actual screen time. Set on the fictional Amity Island, New York, but filmed on Martha's Vineyard, Massachusetts, this shark-cuterie board pays homage to both New England locations with a deconstructed shrimp boil. Enjoy safely inside, far from the beach while watching Brody blast one of the greatest cinema villains of all time into smithereens.

Serves 4

THE BOARD
Mini Old Bay Potatoes

1 pound large tail-on cooked shrimp, defrosted according to package directions, or steam your own fresh

¼ cup clarified or melted butter or ghee

Killerbasa

1 (4.5-ounce) package goat cheese spread

handful of rustic crackers

1 lemon, cut into 8 wedges

1 loaf sourdough bread

finely chopped fresh chives, for sprinkling (optional)

Narragansett lager, to serve

MINI OLD BAY POTATOES
1 pound mini red-skinned potatoes

2 tablespoons extra-virgin olive oil

1 tablespoon Old Bay seasoning

kosher salt, to taste

KILLERBASA
1 tablespoon olive oil

8 ounces kielbasa

THE BOARD
On a large rustic board, place the potatoes, shrimp, butter or ghee, kielbasa, goat cheese spread, and crackers. Serve with lemon wedges and sourdough bread. Sprinkle the goat cheese with chives, if using. Enjoy immediately with Narragansett lager.

MINI OLD BAY POTATOES
Preheat the oven to 425°F. Line a baking sheet with parchment paper.

On the prepared baking sheet, toss the potatoes with the olive oil, Old Bay seasoning, and salt. Bake until fork tender and slightly crispy, about 15 to 20 minutes. Add any extra salt or Old Bay to taste. The potatoes can be served warm or at room temperature.

KILLERBASA
Heat a large pan over medium heat. Add the olive oil, warming it until it shimmers, then add the whole kielbasa. Cook until both sides are golden brown and heated through, about 10 minutes, flipping the sausage about halfway through the cooking time. Place the cooked kielbasa on a cutting board and slice on the bias into ½-inch-thick rings.

PULP STILTON
Pulp Fiction (1994)

Hamburgers are the cornerstone of any nutritious diet. Do you know what they call a quarter pounder with cheese in France? A royale with cheese. What kind of cheese, you may ask? Well, there's nothing like a nice slice of stilton—not melted onto the patty, but added right after the burger has been cooked, so the cheese doesn't lose any of its creamy, subtle sweetness. Sandwich between Hawaiian rolls, and season with pepper and salt for the best g*ddamn burger you've ever had. Oh, and be sure to dip at least one of your fries in the milkshake—it's a pretty f*cking good milkshake.

Serves 4

THE BOARD
Royale with Stilton

1 (16-ounce) package crinkle-cut fries, cooked according to package directions

$5 Shake

condiments, such as ketchup, mustard, and mayo

ROYALE WITH STILTON

1½ pounds 80% lean ground beef

kosher salt, to taste

freshly ground black pepper, to taste

12 Hawaiian rolls or brioche slider buns

3 ounces stilton, crumbled

⅓ cup crispy fried onions

$5 SHAKE
4 cups high-quality vanilla bean ice cream

1 teaspoon vanilla extract

2 cup cold whole milk

whipped cream, as a topping (optional)

4 maraschino cherries, as a topping (optional)

THE BOARD
Place the burgers and fries on a platter, and serve with desired condiments. Pair with the $5 shake or "some damn good coffee."

ROYALE WITH STILTON
Form slider patties by scooping the ground beef with a ¼-cup measuring cup. Make the patties slightly wider than the bun, as the meat will shrink as it cooks. Generously season both sides of the patties with salt and pepper. Cook on a nonstick pan or grill, about 2 minutes per side, or to the desired doneness.

Place each patty on a bun, add about 1 tablespoon of the crumbled cheese, and generously sprinkle with the crispy onions.

$5 SHAKE
Place 4 glasses in the freezer for 10 minutes. Add half of the ice cream, vanilla extract, and milk to a blender, and pulse until desired consistency is reached. Pour into the chilled glasses, and top with whipped cream and a cherry, if you'd like. Repeat with the second half of the ingredients.

Now *this* is a snack board. Nothing says "welcome to Earth" like this summery combination of fresh fruit, deli meats, and cheeses. This savory-sweet smorgasbord of cherries, soppressata, blueberries, and Genoa salami, complemented by the mild flavors of Bayley Hazen Blue and cheese curds, is a testament to the best all of humankind—not just Americans—has to offer. Be sure to enjoy with a cigar *after* the fat lady has sung.

Serves 4

2 ounces Genoa salami, sliced

2 ounces soppressata salami, sliced

4 ounces Bayley Hazen Blue or blue cheese of your choice

7 ounces cheese curds

2 cups cherries

1 pint blueberries

¼ cup honey

¼ cup mixed berry jam

½ cup Marcona almonds

5 ounces star crackers or rustic rosemary crackers of your choice

4 ounces Meyer lemon cookie thins or biscuits of your choice

2 ounces sliced pepper jack or white cheddar, cut into stars using cookie cutters of assorted sizes or cut freehand

On a large round platter or board, overlap slices of Genoa and soppressata salamis in opposing sections throughout the board, and add the blue cheese. Stream large clusters of cheese curds, cherries, and blueberries into open spaces. Add small dishes of honey, jam, and almonds. Overlap crackers and cookies in the remaining open areas. Scatter cheese stars over the board.

THE GOUDAFATHER
The Godfather (1972)

Here's the perfect antipasto meat and cheeseboard to present to a Don when coming to him in friendship. The meatballs and cannoli might even make him forget that you've come to him on his daughter's wedding day. This is an Italian-infused cheeseboard ideal for watching what may be the greatest movie of all time.

Serves 4

THE BOARD
8 ounces pecorino romano

4 ounces double cream gouda, sliced into ¼-inch triangles

1 cup marinated red peppers

1 cup mixed Italian olives

8 slices prosciutto di parma

1 small stick dry Italian salami

8 slices hot sopressata salami

½ Castelvetrano olives

Clemenza's Sunday Sauce

Meatballs and Sausages (see page 98)

½ cup Marcona almonds

handful of breadsticks or crackers

4 cannoli (store-bought is fine)

nice Italian red, to serve

CLEMENZA'S SUNDAY SAUCE
2 (28-ounce) cans whole peeled San Marzano tomatoes

¼ cup extra-virgin olive oil

2 large cloves garlic, crushed

2 tablespoons tomato paste

½ teaspoon sugar, plus more to taste

½ cup red wine

¼ cup water

big pinch of salt, plus more to taste

THE BOARD
Place the pecorino romano on the board, and flake off a few chunks with a cheese fork. Add the gouda triangles to the far section of the board. Place the peppers and olives in small bowls, and scatter them throughout the board. Drape a small mound of prosciutto in an empty corner. Place the stick of salami on the board, and cut a few ⅛-inch-thick slices. Roll or fold the slices of sopressata into quarters, and gently place in the last open section of the board. Make sure no wet ingredients touch the meats or cheeses. Scatter the individual bowls or dishes of meatballs, almonds, breadsticks, and cannoli around the board. Serve with wine and *mangia*!

CLEMENZA'S SUNDAY SAUCE
Empty the canned tomatoes into a large bowl, and crush them with your hands.

In a large heavy-bottomed pot, heat the oil over medium-low heat. When it begins to shimmer, add the crushed garlic and cook until golden, about 5 minutes. Remove the garlic from the pot and discard it. Add the tomato paste and fry until fragrant, about 3 minutes. Add the crushed tomatoes and the sugar, wine, water, and salt. Stir to combine, and bring to a boil over medium heat. Reduce to a simmer and cook uncovered for about 40 minutes, stirring occasionally. Add more salt and sugar to taste.

MEATBALLS AND SAUSAGES

½ pound ground chuck

½ pound ground pork

½ pound ground veal

2 large cloves garlic, finely minced

1 large egg, lightly beaten

3 tablespoons finely chopped parsley, divided

1 cup panko breadcrumbs

1 cup grated parmigiano reggiano, plus more for serving

1 tablespoon kosher salt

freshly ground pepper, to taste

¾ cup water

¼ cup extra-virgin olive oil

3 large sweet Italian sausages

TIP: *Because this recipe makes a large batch of sauce for the meatballs and sausage, feel free to halve it. But since it requires time to prepare, making the whole batch is worthwhile—it freezes well. Conversely, if you don't want to put in the effort, order a few meatballs in sauce from your local Italian restaurant, and boom, the Sunday sauce is served!*

MEATBALLS AND SAUSAGES

While the sauce is simmering, begin preparing the meatballs. Add the ground chuck, pork, and veal, along with the minced garlic, the beaten egg, 2 tablespoons of parsley, the panko, the parmigiano reggiano, and the salt and pepper to a large bowl. Gently combine with your hands, taking care not to overwork the meat and slowly adding water to combine. With wet hands, roll the mixture into 2-inch balls, place on a baking sheet or plate, and put in the fridge.

Heat a large pan over medium heat, then add the oil. When the oil shimmers, add the sweet sausages and brown them on all sides, until mostly cooked through, about 15 minutes. Remove them from the pan, and place on a paper towel–lined plate to cool.

Remove the meatballs from the fridge. In batches, add them to the pan, being careful not to overcrowd the pan. Place the balance of uncooked balls back in the fridge. Brown the meatballs on all sides, about 10 minutes. Continue until all the meatballs are browned, placing cooked batches on a paper towel–lined plate.

Once the sausages have cooled, cut them into 2-inch pieces. Add the sausage slices and meatballs to the Sunday sauce, and simmer uncovered, stirring occasionally, until all the meat is cooked through, about 30 minutes. Add extra salt to taste.

Place in a serving bowl, and top with grated parmigiano reggiano and reserved chopped parsley.

TIP: *Make at least one day ahead, as this recipe gets better over time. Skim any hardened fat from the contents before warming to serve.*

The delightfully rustic food featured on this board is perfect for celebrating a hobbit's birthday or to wrap up and take with you on a long journey to defeat a dark lord. The spread includes some clever "finger-ring" potatoes and is perfect for breakfast, second breakfast, elevensies, luncheon, afternoon tea, dinner, OR supper. Whatever path you choose, make sure to grab a pint of ale before you dig into the one board to rule them all!

Serves 4

THE BOARD

1 (6-ounce) block Basque cheese

½ cold rotisserie chicken, split into parts

"My Precious" Potatoes

2 hard-boiled eggs

1 narrow dried salami of your choice

1 pint figs

handful of rustic crackers or cookies, such as butter almond

½ cup cornichons or mini dill pickles

¼ cup grainy mustard

¼ cup berry jam of your choice

1 cup assorted berries

½ loaf crusty bread

tea or large pints of ale, to serve

"MY PRECIOUS" POTATOES

1 pound creamer potatoes

2 tablespoons olive oil

1 tablespoon finely chopped fresh rosemary

1 teaspoon kosher salt, plus more to taste

freshly ground black pepper, to taste

THE BOARD

On a large serving platter or board, place the cheese in corner of the board and cut a few slices. Add the chicken parts in opposing sections, and cluster the potatoes in another. Place the hard-boiled eggs, salami, figs, crackers or cookies, pickles, and small bowls of mustard and jam in open areas. Scatter berries in any remaining spaces. Serve the bread on the side.

Serve alongside tea or large pints of ale.

"MY PRECIOUS" POTATOES

Preheat the oven to 425°F. Line a baking sheet with parchment paper.

On the prepared baking sheet, toss the potatoes with the olive oil, rosemary, salt, and pepper. Bake until crispy and cooked through, about 15 to 20 minutes, shaking the sheet to toss the potatoes halfway through cooking. Add more salt to taste, and serve warm.

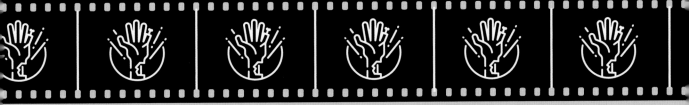

A GOUDA SCARE

HORROR

Evil Dead II: Dead by Dawn (1987)

You may need to recruit another hand to help create this jam-packed snack board filled with ingredients sourced from a haunted fruit cellar. Dried fruit, marmalade, and nuts make up this recipe straight from the Necronomicon. Pay tribute to the cult classic and quintessential horror-comedy *Evil Dead II* by swallowing these snacks before a witch swallows your soul. Your hunger will be dead by dawn.

Serves 8

8 ounces parmesan

1 large bunch red grapes

1 pear, halved, cored, and sliced ¼ inch thick

¼ cup stone-ground mustard

¼ cup apricot jam or marmalade

8 halves dried peaches

¾ cup dried apricots

⅓ cup dried cherries

8 medjool dates

⅓ cup crystalized ginger

8 mini smoked sausages

1 cup crackers, such as fig and rosemary

¾ cup roasted and salted cashews

¾ cup roasted and unsalted almonds

¾ cup roasted and salted pistachios

⅓ cup yogurt-covered raisins

Place the parmesan in the center of the board. Position the bunch of grapes on one side of the board, and the pear slices on the other. Add small bowls of mustard and jam. Begin to add groupings of the dried fruit, dates, ginger, sausage, and crackers around the board. Place the nuts and yogurt-covered raisins in the remaining spaces on the board.

Serve with snack plates, serving utensils for the mustard and jam, and a knife for the cheese.

This board has not been approved by the Vatican. Surely, there is nothing more sacrilegious than taking in the body of Christ after it has been dipped in a sweet pea white bean dip, paired with an assortment of crudités and served on a Ouija board. Perhaps it is a good thing that these are rice crackers and not communion wafers.

Serves 2

THE BOARD
Pazuzu's Dip

1 (3.5-ounce) package rice crackers

assorted crudités, such as 1 small fennel bulb, 4 carrots, and 1 watermelon radish, all thinly sliced, and leaves from 1 small heart of romaine

PAZUZU'S DIP
1 (15-ounce) can cannellini beans, rinsed and drained

1 cup frozen peas, thawed

½ cup packed mint

¼ cup extra-virgin olive oil

juice of 1 large lemon (about 2 tablespoons plus 1 teaspoon)

1 clove garlic, crushed

1 teaspoon kosher salt, plus extra to taste

freshly ground black pepper, to taste

THE BOARD
Pour the dip into a serving bowl and place it on the board. Arrange the crudités and crackers on plates.

PAZUZU'S DIP
To the bowl of a food processor, add the beans, peas, mint, oil, lemon, garlic, salt, and pepper. Puree until smooth. Add extra salt to taste. If the dip is too thick, thin it with extra lemon juice.

TIP: *The dip can be made a day in advance. Just cover it with plastic wrap, making sure the wrap is in contact with the dip, which reduces contact with the air.*

THE SILENCE OF THE LABNEH
The Silence of the Lambs (1991)

Look, no one is trying to tell you what you can and cannot eat. But maybe next time you get the urge to "have a friend for dinner," you can turn to this deliciously disturbing spread instead. Hopefully, the pâté de campagne and fava beans can satisfy any...suspicious cravings you may have. And if you're feeling particularly dangerous, pair this board with a nice chianti.

Serves 2

THE BOARD
4 ounces pâté de campagne (country pork pâté)

1 baguette, sliced ½ inch thick

Labneh Spread

Spring Fava Beans

½ cup olives or cornichons

¼ cup whole grain mustard

nice chianti, to serve

LABNEH SPREAD
1 cup labneh

juice of ½ lemon

drizzle of extra-virgin olive oil

big pinch of salt, plus extra to taste

SPRING FAVA BEANS
1 cup fresh fava beans, shelled, membranes removed, and blanched

zest of 1 lemon

1 tablespoon finely chopped mint

2 teaspoons extra-virgin olive oil, plus extra for finishing

¼ teaspoon kosher salt, plus extra to taste

freshly ground pepper, to taste

THE BOARD
For this tapas-style take on "I ate his liver with some fava beans and a nice chianti," place all the ingredients in small bowls or on small plates, and arrange them on a board or large tray, along with appetizer plates for serving. If you have a spreader that resembles a dagger or other dangerous-looking serving tools, so much the better.

Let your guests enjoy the components on their own or combined. The labneh is great on a baguette and topped with fava beans. The pâté is also tasty on the baguette with a smear of mustard and a nibble of cornichon.

LABNEH SPREAD
Mix all the ingredients together in a small bowl, and add any extra salt or lemon juice to taste.

SPRING FAVA BEANS
Place all the ingredients in a small bowl and toss to combine. Add any extra salt to taste, and finish with a drizzle of olive oil. Serve immediately.

"ALL WORK AND NO WHEY MAKES JACK A DULL BOY"

The Shining (1980)

The finest the Overlook Hotel has to offer for a much-needed writing break, this snack board provides a delicious selection of cheeses and chocolate. Grab a seat by the bar and Lloyd will pour you a glass of hair of the dog, perhaps a bourbon on the rocks or a manhattan like the one below. This pairing should help you fend off cabin fever, ghostly twins, bloody elevators, and whatever is haunting room 237.

Serves 1

THE BOARD

1 ounce aged gouda, sliced

1 ounce stilton

1 ounce triple crème brie

1 bar dark chocolate, broken into large chunks

Maniac's Manhattan, to serve

MANIAC'S MANHATTAN

2 ounces bourbon

1 ounce sweet vermouth

2 dashes angostura bitters

1 maraschino cherry, for garnish

THE BOARD

Place the cheeses and chocolate on a small plate, and serve alongside the manhattan.

MANIAC'S MANHATTAN

Combine the bourbon, vermouth, and bitters. Stir and strain into a chilled cocktail glass and garnish with a maraschino cherry.

THE NIGHTMARE BEFORE CHARCUTERIE
The Nightmare before Christmas (1993)

What's this? There's candy everywhere. What's this? The scent of cheese is in the air. Just as the classic stop-motion musical blends two different holiday seasons, this twist on a charcuterie board offers savory and sweet treats perfect for Christmas or Halloween. In place of a traditional board are personal charcuterie cups perfect for every good child (and kid-at-heart) on Santa's list. Keep Oogie Boogie away by creating your very own Jack Skellington cookies!

Makes 8

JACK SKELLINGTON CHARCUTERIE CUPS

½ cup black candy melts

8 mini black and white cookies (about 8 ounces)

½ cup yogurt-covered raisins

½ cup chocolate-covered raisins or nuts

½ cup mixed nuts

1 (1.41-ounce) package Pocky cookies and cream

2 types (4 ounces each) salami of your choice, thinly sliced

JACK SKELLINGTON CHARCUTERIE CUPS

In the microwave, melt the black candy melts according to package directions. Place the cookies on a plate or tray. Transfer the melted chocolate to a zip-top bag, and snip off the tip very close to the edge. Pipe the chocolate onto the cookies to look like Jack Skellington's face. Place the cookies in the fridge to harden, about 20 minutes.

TIP: *You can decorate and harden the cookies in the fridge the day before.*

You will need 8 small juice glasses or jars. Add about 2 tablespoons each of the yogurt-covered raisins and the chocolate-covered raisins or nuts to each glass or jar, and mix to combine. Add a stick of Pocky to each.

You will also need 8 skewers or picks. Fold the salami slices in quarters, and push them onto the skewers, about a third of the way down. Rotate the two salami types, so you end up with four slices of salami on each skewer. Top with a decorated black and white cookie. Place a skewered figure in each glass or jar, then arrange all of them on a large platter.

Drink of your sisters and take into yourself this delicious four-part board that represents four different corners needed to invoke the spirit of your choice, but be careful who you summon. While Kraft brand cheese doesn't actually make an appearance on the board, the Midnight Moon (aged gouda) is a much tastier and witchier replacement. Blessed be!

Serves 4

THE BOARD

8 ounces mixed nuts

Midnight Moon cheese or aged gouda, sliced lengthwise into wedges

8 ounces sriracha peas

Watchtower Pretzel Fish

WATCHTOWER PRETZEL FISH

1 (8-ounce) package pretzel goldfish crackers

1 tablespoon unsalted butter

3 tablespoons dark brown sugar

¼ teaspoon cinnamon

¼ teaspoon cayenne

1 tablespoon maple syrup

¾ teaspoon unsweetened cocoa powder

¼ teaspoon kosher salt

THE BOARD

On a serving tray with four sections, add the nuts, cheese, and sriracha peas, along with the sweet and savory pretzel fish.

WATCHTOWER PRETZEL FISH

Preheat the oven to 300°F and line a baking sheet with parchment paper. Place the pretzel goldfish crackers on the sheet. Set aside.

In a small saucepan, melt the butter over low heat. Then add the brown sugar, cinnamon, cayenne, maple syrup, cocoa powder, and salt, and whisk to combine. Remove from the heat, and drizzle the mixture over the crackers, tossing with a spatula until evenly coated.

Bake for about 12 minutes, tossing about midway through. Remove from the oven and allow to cool completely, about 15 minutes. Break up any clumps and serve.

THE ROQUEFORT HORROR PICTURE SHOW
The Rocky Horror Picture Show (1975)

This board would like, if it may, to take you on a strange journey. A journey full of dark humor, questionable science, and outstanding musical numbers all wrapped up in mini meat loafs (R.I.P. Eddie), cheeses, jams, fruit, and more. By the end, you'll feel like embracing your wacky and fabulous self, just as the good Dr. Frank-N-Furter ordered.

Serves 4

THE BOARD

4 ounces roquefort cheese

3.5 ounces mini kunik, or a small wheel of brie

¼ cup red berry jam

8 slices prosciutto

Mini Meat Loaves (see page 118)

1 pint strawberries

½ pint raspberries

½ pint blackberries

4 ounces black licorice

handful of olive oil and sea salt sourdough crackers or crackers of your choice

THE BOARD

On a tray or platter, place the cheeses across from each other, and position the jam near the kunik or brie. Drape the prosciutto into an open space, and place the meat loaves in the last large open area. Fill in any remaining open spots with an arrangement of berries, licorice, and crackers, playing up the red and black vibes.

MINI MEAT LOAVES
Meat Loaf
1 pound ground beef

½ cup finely crushed Ritz crackers

2 tablespoons minced garlic

2 tablespoons soy sauce

1 teaspoon sesame oil

1 tablespoon brown sugar

1 teaspoon kosher salt

1 tablespoon water

Glaze
1 tablespoon gochujang

1 teaspoon mirin

1 teaspoon brown sugar

½ teaspoon sesame oil

1 teaspoon soy sauce

1 teaspoon rice wine vinegar

MINI MEAT LOAVES
Preheat the oven to 425°F. Line a baking sheet with parchment paper, and set aside.

In a large bowl, combine all the ingredients for the meat loaves, using your hands to combine, but not overmix.

With damp hands, roll about ¼ cup of the meatloaf mixture into a ball, place on the baking sheet , and mold into an oval meat loaf shape. Exaggerate the oval shape, as the meat can seize up in the oven and retract to a rounder shape.

In a small bowl, whisk together all the ingredients for the glaze. Brush or spoon the glaze over the meat loaves.

Bake until cooked through and golden brown around the edges, about 15 to 20 minutes. Serve warm. Makes 12 loaves.

TIP: *The meat loaves can be assembled the night before and baked the day they'll be served.*

NOTE: *The Mini Meat Loaves recipe was inspired by Kay Chun's Korean BBQ–Style Meatballs recipe for* The New York Times.

CHEESY GOUDA FUN

COMEDY

"SHE TURNED ME INTO CRUDITÉS! ... I GOT BETTER"

Monty Python and the Holy Grail (1975)

This shrubbery-inspired board is good to have on hand if you ever encounter the Knights Who Say Ni (or the Knights Who 'Til Recently Said Ni). Fresh vegetables and a little cracker path running down the middle are sure to please even the most discerning of knights, and you can continue on to seek the Holy Grail.

Serves 4

1 package square crackers of your choice, such as raisin rosemary crisps

10 ounces dip of your choice, such as pesto hummus

¼ small head red cabbage, quartered

1 (.35-ounce) package roasted seaweed snacks

6 ounces baby zucchini, sliced in half lengthwise

6 ounces baby cauliflower

8 ounces multicolored cauliflower florets

1 Granny Smith apple, halved, cored, and thinly sliced

2 ounces kale chips

¼ cup coconut chips

On a large platter or tray, lay the crackers in a winding, overlapping path. Transfer the dip to a small bowl and place it on the platter or tray, nestled up to the cracker path. Add clusters of the cabbage and seaweed snacks, and groupings of the zucchini and cauliflower in the large open spaces. Fan out small groupings of the sliced apple, and tuck them into small spaces. Sprinkle the kale chips and coconut chips in any last free nooks.

SOME LIKE IT HABANERO
Some Like It Hot (1959)

Witness a mafia hit? No need to join Sweet Sue and Her Society Syncopators—instead you can hide out at home with this delightfully spicy cheese plate. But if you'd like to slip on a wig and pretend to be a saxophonist, no one will stop you. This 1959 rom-com classic starring Marilyn Monroe, Tony Curtis, and Jack Lemmon is a gem, and it's responsible, in part, for doing away with the Hays Code, which censored "undesirable" content in Hollywood. Fake millionaires may prefer the classic flavors, but the rich-at-heart prefer flamin' hot cheetos!

Serves 4

4 ounces hot capicola or hot sopressata salami

1 (8-ounce) block fiesta pepper jack or any pepper jack, sliced ¼ inch thick, then cut diagonally

½ cup sweet and spicy Peppadew peppers

1 (8-ounce) block habanero cheddar, sliced ¼ inch thick

6 ounces chile-spiced dried pineapple

¼ cup hot chile honey

½ cup pistachios, or nuts of your choice

7 ounces cheese curds

1 (3.5-ounce) bag Flaming' Hot Cheetos

1 (1.7-ounce) package jalapeño parmesan crisps

4 ounces mild and crispy crackers of your choice

big glass of water or a cold tall one, to serve

Drape the capicola onto the lower corner of the board, and fan the points of the pepper jack around the capicola cluster. Place a small bowl of the Peppadew peppers on the opposite upper section. Fan slices of the habanero cheddar around the bowl, and drape the dried pineapple around the cheddar. Add a small bowl of the honey along with groupings of pistachios, cheese curds, and Cheetos to open areas. Place the parmesan crisps and the crackers in the last open spots. Serve with water or a cold beer to curb the heat.

CHEDDARLESS

Clueless (1995)

To thine own self be true! Whether you need a quick snack before your driving test or a reward for successfully negotiating higher grades, look no further than a turkey sandwich, carrot sticks, five peanut butter M&M's, licorice sticks, and a can of diet soda.

Serves 4

8 slices sourdough bread

1 pound boneless turkey breast, thinly sliced

½ pound sharp cheddar

lettuce

1 large tomato, sliced

mayo

1 (1.63-ounce) bag peanut butter M&M's

12 Twizzlers or any licorice sticks

1 pound carrots, cut into sticks

4 cherry Blow Pops

4 (7.5-fluid ounce) cans Diet Coke, to serve

Assemble the bread, turkey, cheddar, lettuce, tomato, and mayo into 4 sandwiches. Slice in half and place on plates, along with the carrot sticks. Serve with 5 peanut butter M&M's, 3 Twizzlers, 1 Blow Pop, and a can of Diet Coke for each guest.

NACHOS LIBRE

Nacho Libre (2006)

Who doesn't want a small taste of glory? With a little determination, hard work, and a few lucha libre wrestling moves, you, too, can whip up this board of spectacular nachos that are sure to bring glory and honor to all who eat them. So put on your favorite stretchy pants and get cooking!

Serves 4

THE BOARD

1 (12-ounce) bag white corn tortilla chips

Barbacoa Brisket (see page 128)

1 (15-ounce) can black beans, rinsed and drained

1 (8-ounce) bag shredded sharp cheddar jack cheese

Quick Pico (see page 129)

1 (11-ounce) can pickled jalapeño peppers

2 tablespoons chopped cilantro, for sprinkling

Lime Crema (see page 129)

THE BOARD

Preheat the oven to 350°F. Line a baking sheet with parchment paper or spray a nonstick baking sheet with cooking spray, and set aside.

Arrange half of the tortilla chips on the prepared baking sheet, and top with half of the Barbacoa Brisket, beans, and shredded cheese. Repeat with the remaining chips, Barbacoa Brisket, beans, and shredded cheese.

Bake until the cheese is melted, about 20 minutes. Top with some of the quick pico and pickled jalapeño peppers, and sprinkle on the cilantro. Drizzle with Lime Crema. Serve with the remaining pico and pickled jalapeño peppers in individual small bowls, and with lime wedges on the side.

BARBACOA BRISKET

3 to 4 pounds brisket

kosher salt, to taste, for seasoning brisket and marinade

freshly ground black pepper, to taste, for seasoning brisket and marinade

4 dried ancho peppers, stemmed and seeded

4 dried guajillo peppers, stemmed and seeded

4 dried arbol chiles, stemmed and seeded

6 cups water, divided

⅓ cup apple cider vinegar

½ large yellow onion, quartered

4 cloves garlic

3 canned chipotle peppers, plus 2 tablespoons adobo sauce

1 tablespoon tomato paste

1 tablespoon dried oregano

½ teaspoon cumin

½ teaspoon cinnamon

¼ teaspoon dried thyme

¼ teaspoon ground cloves

juice of ½ lime

lime wedges, for serving

BARBACOA BRISKET

Pat dry the brisket, and season generously with salt and pepper. Set aside.

Heat a large saucepan over medium heat. Add the dried peppers and chiles and toast, turning continuously, until fragrant, about 3 minutes. Add 5 cups of water, and cook until the peppers and chiles are soft, about 12 minutes.

Transfer the peppers and chiles to a blender or food processor, along with 2 cups of the cooking liquid. Add the vinegar, onion, garlic, chipotles and adobo sauce, tomato paste, oregano, cumin, cinnamon, thyme, and cloves, along with salt and pepper to taste. Puree until smooth for the most beautiful red, fragrant marinade.

In a large Dutch oven, add the brisket, fat side up, along with the marinade mixture, making sure the brisket is completely covered with the marinade. Marinate for at least 2 hours or overnight.

Add 1 cup of water to the marinated brisket in the Dutch oven and bring to a boil over medium-high heat. Once bubbling, reduce the heat to medium-low and simmer, cooking covered for about 3 hours, or 2 hours per pound, basting every 30 minutes. When down to the last hour, add 1 tablespoon of salt and the lime juice.

Once the brisket has cooled, completely remove the fat cap, and pull or shred as much of the meat as you like for the nacho dish. Keep the leftover brisket whole for slicing into sandwiches.

TIP: *Barbacoa Brisket is best prepared the day before and kept overnight in the fridge to let the flavors meld. Before warming, remove any orange fat that has collected at the surface.*

QUICK PICO

2 medium tomatoes, seeded and diced

½ medium onion, diced

1 medium jalapeño pepper, seeded and finely diced

¼ cup chopped cilantro

juice of ½ lime

½ teaspoon kosher salt, plus more to taste

LIME CREMA

8 ounces sour cream

juice of 1 lime (about 2 tablespoons)

½ teaspoon kosher salt, plus more to taste

QUICK PICO

In a medium bowl, combine all the ingredients and add extra salt to taste. Serve immediately.

LIME CREMA

Add all ingredients to a small bowl and stir to combine. The mixture should be pourable and not too thick. If it needs to be thinned, add more lime juice. Add extra salt to taste.

TIP: *The Lime Crema can be made up to a day ahead of time and kept covered in the fridge.*

FERRIS BEER-CHEESE'S DAY OFF

Ferris Bueller's Day Off (1986)

You're trying to decide what to eat for lunch. If you played by the rules, you'd only be able to eat one thing. But why pick one lunch food when you can have the whole lot? Who cares what you had for dinner last night? Life's too short to be counting calories! Go out and have all the deep-dish pizza and hot dogs you want! You're only young once—who knows what your metabolism will be like after college.

Serves 4

1 package beef hot dogs

1 package Chicago-style hot dog buns with poppy seeds or hot dog buns of your choice

1 Chicago-style deep-dish pizza, cooked according to package directions

4 kosher-style pickles, quartered lengthwise into spears

2 plum tomatoes, halved lengthwise and sliced ¼ inch thick

1 small white onion, diced

½ cup sport peppers, or any small hot peppers

½ cup giardiniera

¼ cup yellow mustard

½ cup green relish

6 cups Chicago-style popcorn (half cheddar, half caramel corn)

celery salt, for sprinkling

Fill a medium saucepan three-quarters full with water, bring to a boil, then reduce to a simmer. Add the hot dogs and simmer until hot, about 5 minutes. In a steamer basket or strainer set over the simmering water, steam the buns for about 2 minutes.

On a large tray or serving platter, add the hot dogs, buns, and pizza. Add the pickle spears, preferably away from the buns and pizza, to reduce moisture. Place the tomatoes, onion, peppers, giardiniera, mustard, and relish in small bowls, and scatter them on the board. Scatter the popcorn in open spaces, or serve it on the side in a large bowl. Place a jar of celery salt on the side.

KENNY'S SWEET MUNCHIE BOARD
Half-Baked (1998)

You and your friends have just smoked some of the best sh*t on the planet. You're on snack duty. Nothing slays the munchies like wavy potato chips, Funyuns, gummy bears, marshmallows, graham crackers, chocolate, s'mores, celery with grape jelly, sour cream and onion dip, pink popcorn, and pizza. Bonus points if you can even find an Abba-Zaba. Just don't give any of this to a diabetic police horse.

Serves 4

1 ginormous bag wavy potato chips

10 ounces sour cream and onion dip

4 stalks celery, cut horizontally in thirds

⅓ cup grape jelly

6 cups pink popcorn

1 bag Funyuns

1 sleeve graham crackers

2 cups marshmallows

2 (6-ounce) Hershey's chocolate bars

1 cup gummy bears, or beef jerky as requested in the movie

water, a whole lotta water, to serve

On a large tray, place the potato chips and a small bowl containing the dip in one corner, and the celery stalks and the jelly in a small bowl in the other. In the opposite corners, add the popcorn and the Funyuns. In the center, scatter the graham crackers, marshmallows, and chocolate. Add the gummy bears or beef jerky to the last remaining area. If a couple of big pizzas happen to show up, you know what to do with them.

THE BIG LEBLEUCHEESE
The Big Lebowski (1998)

F*ck it, Dude, let's get wings. Whether you're getting ready to throw some rocks or just kick back with a j and your recording of the *Venice Beach League Playoffs 1987*, here's the fare for you. No night hitting strikes is complete without mozz sticks, waffle fries, and all the necessary dips. Finally, careful, man, there's beverage here—so don't forget the half and half.

Serves 2

THE BOARD

1 (16-ounce) bag Buffalo chicken tenders, cooked according to package directions

4 stalks celery, cut into sticks

12 ounces waffle fries, cooked according to package directions

1 (8-ounce) bag mozzarella sticks, cooked according to package directions

1 (13.5-ounce) bag onion rings, cooked according to package directions

⅓ cup blue cheese dressing

⅓ cup marinara sauce

⅓ cup ketchup

⅓ cup ranch dressing

2 White Russians, to serve

WHITE RUSSIAN

1½ ounces Kahlúa

1 ounce vodka

1 ounce heavy whipping cream

THE BOARD

In a basket with a liner, place the chicken tenders, celery, and waffle fries. Add the mozzarella sticks and onion rings to a second basket. Put all the sauces in small dipping bowls, and serve alongside their corresponding snacks. Accompany with white Russians.

WHITE RUSSIAN

Fill a rocks glass with ice, and add the Kahlúa and vodka. Stir briefly. Top with heavy whipping cream, and serve. Makes 1.

NOTE: *The White Russian recipe is from the book* Mixology and Murder *by Kierra Sondereker.*

Don't you forget about the most important meal of the day. No pun needed here since this is literally a breakfast board, although totally suitable for eating at any time of day you start to stream this coming-of-age classic. Fresh fruit, homemade mini tarts, cereal mix, and Pixy Stix are essential for surviving your nine-hour Saturday detention. All two months of them.

Serves 4

THE BOARD

1 package waffle sticks, prepared according to package directions

syrup of your choice

Homemade Mini Tarts (see page 138)

assorted fruit of your choice

8 Pixy Stix

Basket Case Cereal Mix (see page 138)

milk or orange juice, to serve

THE BOARD

Place the waffle sticks, Homemade Mini Tarts, assorted fruit, Pixy Stix, and cereal mix on one or more serving trays. Pair with milk or orange juice.

HOMEMADE MINI TARTS

1 pie crust, thawed according to package directions and flattened

¼ cup strawberry jam

½ cup powdered sugar

1 to 2 tablespoons milk

⅛ teaspoon vanilla extract

red food coloring

sprinkles (optional)

BASKET CASE CEREAL MIX

1 cup Lucky Charms

1 cup Trix

1 cup Cinnamon Toast Crunch

1 cup Cocoa Puffs

HOMEMADE MINI TARTS

Preheat the oven to 400°F. Line a baking sheet with parchment paper, and set aside.

Roll out the pie crust between two layers of plastic wrap or wax paper to approximately 8 x 9 inches. If the crust is circular, fold in the round edges to make a rectangular shape and roll until you have the dimensions you want. Along the longest side, cut strips 2 inches apart, then cut strips crosswise 1½ inches apart. You should have 24 rectangles.

Add ¼ teaspoon jam to the center of each of 12 rectangles, then top with the remaining 12 rectangles. Crimp the edges with a fork to seal the layers, and place them 1 inch apart on the baking sheet.

TIP: *If the dough gets sticky to work with, pop it in the freezer for about 5 or 10 minutes to firm up.*

Bake until golden brown, 15 to 20 minutes. Set aside to cool, then move the individual tarts to a cooling rack after about 5 minutes.

In a small bowl, combine the powdered sugar, 1 tablespoon of milk, the vanilla, and the food coloring, and stir to combine. If the glaze is too thick to pour, add the remaining milk, a small amount at a time, until you have the desired consistency.

Once the tarts are cool, drizzle or spoon glaze over them and top with the sprinkles, if using. Set aside to let the glaze set before serving. Makes 12 tarts.

BASKET CASE CEREAL MIX

Place all the ingredients in a medium bowl and toss to combine.

TIP: *Feel free to use any cereal of your liking!*

CONVERSIONS

VOLUME

US	US Equivalent	Metric
1 tablespoon (3 teaspoons)	½ fluid ounce	15 milliliters
¼ cup	2 fluid ounces	60 milliliters
⅓ cup	3 fluid ounces	90 milliliters
½ cup	4 fluid ounces	120 milliliters
⅔ cup	5 fluid ounces	150 milliliters
¾ cup	6 fluid ounces	180 milliliters
1 cup	8 fluid ounces	240 milliliters
2 cups	16 fluid ounces	480 milliliters

WEIGHT

US	Metric
½ ounce	15 grams
1 ounce	30 grams
2 ounces	60 grams
¼ pound	115 grams
⅓ pound	150 grams
½ pound	225 grams
¾ pound	350 grams
1 pound	450 grams

TEMPERATURE

Fahrenheit (°F)	Celsius (°C)	Fahrenheit (°F)	Celsius (°C)
70°F	20°C	220°F	105°C
100°F	40°C	240°F	115°C
120°F	50°C	260°F	125°C
130°F	55°C	280°F	140°C
140°F	60°C	300°F	150°C
150°F	65°C	325°F	165°C
160°F	70°C	350°F	175°C
170°F	75°C	375°F	190°C
180°F	80°C	400°F	200°C
190°F	90°C	425°F	220°C
200°F	95°C	450°F	230°C

RECIPE AND MOVIE INDEX

ACKNOWLEDGMENTS

I want to thank my friends and family for their constant love, support, and snack ideas. Additionally, I'd like to thank my mom and mother-in-law for letting me raid their cabinets and pottery collections for unique props and serving pieces to help bring this consistently inconsistent project to life.

Kourtney, for helping me land the first of hopefully many book projects and, more importantly, for your unwavering friendship. Casie, Shelona, and the team at Ulysses Press for the opportunity to combine my passion for food, photography, and styling and for the guidance provided during the process.

Most importantly, Evan, thank you for your support with this project and for rewatching all the childhood classics and rom-coms, like *When Harry Met Sally*, when all you want to do was chill and watch baseball at the end of a long day. Also, for the constant brainstorming and helping me bring your *Half Baked* stoner snack fantasy to life. And to Charlie, for being the most amazingly bright and wonderful little guy a parent could ask for, I love you more than words express.

I hope everyone reading this gets a few friends together (it's been too long!) and has a great time creating a snack board to munch on while watching one of your favorite flicks.

Peace, love, and prosciutto, Rachel.

ABOUT THE CREATOR

Rachel Riederman is a fashion designer turned food stylist and photographer. After almost two decades in corporate fashion, she was inspired to change careers and follow her passion for all things food and entertaining. As a home cook, Riederman uses seasonal ingredients to craft easy, accessible recipes. She's a travel enthusiast (Morocco is next on her list of countries to visit) and always first in line to try the newest restaurants in NYC. Now a city girl planted in the suburbs, Riederman lives just outside NYC with her husband, toddler son Charlie, and Siamese cats, Murphy and Smooch. This is her first book. For more food and recipe inspiration, follow her on Instagram at @whatsinrachelskitchen.